Mountain Lines

Mountain Lines

A Journey through the French Alps

Jonathan Arlan

Skyhorse Publishing

Copyright © 2017 by Jonathan Arlan

All rights reserved. No part of this book may be reproduced in any manner without the express written consent of the publisher, except in the case of brief excerpts in critical reviews or articles. All inquiries should be addressed to Skyhorse Publishing, 307 West 36th Street, 11th Floor, New York, NY 10018.

Skyhorse Publishing books may be purchased in bulk at special discounts for sales promotion, corporate gifts, fund-raising, or educational purposes. Special editions can also be created to specifications. For details, contact the Special Sales Department, Skyhorse Publishing, 307 West 36th Street, 11th Floor, New York, NY 10018 or info@skyhorsepublishing.com.

Skyhorse® and Skyhorse Publishing® are registered trademarks of Skyhorse Publishing, Inc.®, a Delaware corporation.

Visit our website at www.skyhorsepublishing.com.

10 9 8 7 6 5 4 3 2 1

Library of Congress Cataloging-in-Publication Data is available on file.

Cover design by Zach Arlan
Cover photo credit: Jonathan Arlan

Print ISBN: 978-1-5107-0975-1
Ebook ISBN: 978-1-5107-0976-8

Printed in the United States of America

To my father, brother, sister, and, most of all, my mother.

"Beware thoughts that come in the night."
—William Least Heat-Moon, *Blue Highways*

"Why then was I attracted to it? There are ideas which link together, flow on and gradually impose themselves."
—Gaston Rébuffat, *Starlight and Storm*

Mountain Lines

Prologue

I should say up front that, as far as grand adventure stories go, mine is neither especially grand—at least in terms of distance traveled—nor all that adventurous. There are people out there, truly adventurous souls who, for reasons I doubt I'll ever understand, dream up absurdly punishing things to do with their bodies and with their time—people who cross deserts on foot in 120-degree heat; people who hack their way through jungles while tiny insects eat away at their eyeballs; people who float across shark-infested oceans on rafts; people who, at great personal risk, slip quietly into war zones to report back to the rest of us. I am not one of those people, not by any measurement under the sun; I have no desire to stare death in the eye, to put myself in harm's way, to scrape down and find the pleasure on the other side of pain. So while these are the stories I love to read, they are not the stories I can write.

I can write, however, about walking—which, I'll admit, may seem a boring subject to most, though not to me. And I can write about a tiny corner of southeastern France; about being outside of my world and wildly out of my element; about pain; about solitude and loneliness and companionship; and, to a small degree, about nature. In a lovely sketch of the Tyrolean Alps, the novelist James Salter writes of a "journey that follows a journey and leads one through days of almost mindless exertion and unpunished joy." He's talking about skiing, but in my mind at least he could just as easily be talking about any kind of travel—driving, or flying, or sailing, or running. Or, why not, even walking.

All of which is to say I can really only write about my own journey—a small, slow, low-risk adventure with many days of mindless exertion and a few of unpunished joy, a journey through one of the most stunningly gorgeous and surprising and storied slivers of land on the planet.

It starts like this:

Just as the sun was coming up on a chilly early-August morning, I took the first of roughly one million steps on a walk that would lead me from the southern lip of Lake Geneva, through a large swath of the French Alps, and finally to the Mediterranean Sea, where it would have been impossible to walk any farther. People sometimes speak of moments in their lives when, in an instant, everything changes, and it's very possible that that first step was one of those moments. Of course, it's also possible that it was just the first of far too many steps on a path I had no real business being on, a path I knew almost nothing about, a path I was totally unprepared for—a journey I hadn't earned.

But if you could see it happen—if you could watch my right foot fall toward the ground in slow motion and freeze time in the split second before it lands, with the rubber tread of my hiking boot hovering just over the earth—you might see a line, a hair-thin thread of light that, once crossed, will divide my life in two. There is the old me: lazy, indecisive, afraid; and the new: resolute, brave, daring. In a word, adventurous.

Unfortunately, none of this occurred to me at the time. I was far too preoccupied with figuring out (a) what it was I had committed myself to, (b) how I ended up there, alone in the foothills of the Alps, and (c) just how bad of an idea it was to put any real thoughts in any real order. To be honest, what I felt most acutely in that moment—and in the days and weeks leading up to it—was dread. I couldn't have pinpointed the origins of that feeling, but it was dread all right, pure and potent and, at times, paralyzing. It's only in retrospect that the scene acquires the glow and gravity of a Profound Moment, a spiritual moment. A miracle, even.

For fun, though, and because memories are endlessly malleable and always changing, here is what it looks like in the syrupy light of my own head: The morning is unnaturally quiet, close to silent, and still, like the inside of an empty church. The cool, fresh scents of the mountain blow by me and I fill my lungs with the buoyant, life-giving air. I take the first step. I close that initial gap between myself and the earth, putting the ground firmly beneath me. I pause. Then I take a dozen more steps. Then a hundred more, and when the number gets high enough, I laugh at my childish scorekeeping, and I stop counting.

The ground is soft from several days of rain and my shoes sink down and spring up with each step. Walking out of the small town where I slept the night before, I see an old man who notices my pack and walking poles and excitedly wishes me *bonne chance*. I wonder if he knows how far I'm going.

On the edge of the woods, a small dog watches me. He holds my eyes for a beat before I turn and disappear into the trees.

The knot in my stomach, which has cinched tighter and tighter over the last few days, loosens ever so slightly with each step, like a constrictor finally exhausted from the effort of suffocating its next meal.

There's an image, too—one I come back to again and again, one (I swear) I actually had in my head at the time: an astronaut. He drifts slowly through space attached to the end of a tether. It looks like he's barely moving, but the cord that connects him the to the craft, to the earth, to everything, is tightening, losing slack. The line stretches and stretches and stretches until, silently, it snaps. Melodramatic? Sure, but that's what it felt like that morning to walk slowly out of a place to which I had no intention of ever returning—like floating.

Or drifting.

Part One
Wandering

1

When I was a kid, perhaps in first or second grade, I was obsessed with maps. I could stare at them for hours memorizing the names of countries, capitals, rivers, and mountains, trying to cram and hold as many six-point-type details into my head as I could. The way some children can lose themselves in the minutiae of baseball cards, or video games, or stories about magicians and dragons, I could lose myself in maps.

I'd start with the big places—Russia, China, Canada—and fill in the blanks. South America was easy with its nice, chunky countries and pretty names. Europe east of Germany was a little trickier, all nervous borders and ever-shrinking republics. And Africa was impossible, too big, too thick with jungles and savannahs and deserts. But every once in a while, all the pieces would click into place, fall together like a jigsaw puzzle, and for short, bright moments I could close my eyes and picture the entire world framed in a perfect rectangle. I knew who shared borders with whom, and where Tibet was, and that there was a place called Elephant Island near Antarctica. I even knew the oceans and seas and lakes, the negative spaces that held everything in its proper place.

I loved the tiny countries especially, the ones you really had to look for: Andorra, squeezed between Spain and France; Vatican City, hiding in the middle of Rome; Mauritius, way down next to Madagascar, smaller than my fingernail. For a child as consumed as I was, these were the discoveries that turned any page with lines, land, and a compass rose map into a treasure map.

I can remember a map we had on our classroom wall. It was old and neglected, left over from the Cold War. Huge sections of it were totally obsolete. I must have been eight or nine. Faintly, I can see the lamination peeling back at the corners and each country in a different color: pink, yellow, green. The oceans are the exact color a child thinks of when he hears the word "blue"; Antarctica is snow white. When you're young you wonder if Morocco really is the pale pink color of flamingoes. If Australia is mustard yellow. You trace the Nile with your index finger from the top of Africa, through Egypt, through Sudan, to somewhere in the middle, a lake, but you can never remember the name of it. You draw connections between words you've heard somewhere, like Baghdad or Jerusalem or Bosnia, and places that actually exist, places you can point to, places you can *go* to. You wish that Alaska and Russia would touch because then it would at least be possible to walk around the world. Starting at the tip of Argentina, you would go up through the Amazon, through Mexico, Canada, Alaska, across Russia, into Europe, and down to the bottom of Africa. You could circumnavigate (a new word) the globe on foot; you could do it without ever leaving the ground.

8

You never look at America, because it's all one color (except for the dirty white smudge where you live, smack in the center) and it seems like everywhere else there are places with names that barely sound real: Czechoslovakia, Yugoslavia, Zaire, Bhutan.

In my mind, the map is huge, wider than my wingspan. It holds the entire world. But when I think about it, it's not nearly big enough. Maps, even the huge ones, have no choice but to render everything in them maddeningly small. Still, it's thrilling, getting lost in this map in particular. Time disappears when I do, when I think about how long and thin Chile is, how lonely Tahiti is out there in the middle of the sea, how many places there are. At the bottom, where the paper curls from being rolled up all the time, are the flags of every country in the world, in alphabetical order. Every country in the world in perfect rows and columns, like a checklist.

It's impossible, I think, to read stories of other people's adventures and not want an adventure for yourself. At least for me it is. If I so much as glimpse a headline about an archeologist digging in the Gobi Desert, a hiker lost in the Yukon, or a woman sailing alone around the world; or if I read a dispatch in a magazine from someone canoeing down the Mississippi or hopping trains across Central Asia, I become possessed, briefly, by the idea of dropping everything to go on some grand adventure—travel Africa top to bottom, move to Cambodia, cycle across Siberia. Sometimes the names of certain places—Krakatoa, Karakoram, Kamchatka—alone are enough to absolutely hypnotize me. All of a sudden, I need to move. It's a potent feeling, like a drug. And just like with a drug, the feeling inevitably wears off and I'm left with the crushing reality that, for a thousand small reasons, I will probably never cross a desert on a camel, summit a mountain, or hitchhike the Silk Route.

The problem, or one problem (there are many), is that I'm an intensely lazy person. But like all lazy people I'm easily seduced by romantic visions of myself as an emphatically nonlazy person, a real go-getter, someone who fixes motorcycles, researches indigenous tribes in Papua New Guinea, owns a company selling rare coffee beans, and has a side gig as a conflict photographer. Clearly I'm doing something wrong, sitting here at a desk, tapping on a computer, reading about other people's exciting lives.

Still, I love adventure stories; I can't get enough of them. But I read them jealously. I think: It should be me out there. Or rather, why shouldn't it be me out there? What do these "adventurers" have that I don't? What do they *know* that I don't? I remember reading Bruce Chatwin's *In Patagonia* as a teenager in Kansas. Most of the book, with its enigmatic atmosphere that I would come to love later on, went over my head at the time, but the idea of leaving a boring career behind to travel alone to one of the most remote regions of the world made perfect, profound sense.

But just because I "got it" did not mean I knew what to do with it. Which is not to say I haven't traveled, just that it never feels like I'm doing it right. The truth is, in my own languid way, I've gone after adventure—small, safe doses of it, anyway—whenever the opportunity arose. As a student, I spent half a year living in Cairo—which is to the Kansas City suburb where I grew up what the lost city of El Dorado is to the El Dorado you can easily find in southern Kansas (pronounced el-dor-ay-do, population thirteen thousand). The university put me up in a roach-infested hotel on the west side of the Nile, which meant crossing the river twice a day to get to school and back. For the equivalent of a dollar or two, I could take a black-and-white taxi all the way to Tahrir Square, where the university was located. Depending on traffic, the drive took anywhere from fifteen minutes to two hours. In the summer heat, any exposed skin stuck to the seat and after a few minutes it was like being rolled slowly through an industrial oven. When the drivers spoke English, or felt like wading through my Arabic, they loved chatting. They would complain in tight, tourist-English phrases about Mubarak (who was still in power), or gush at length about their families and their kids who spoke three languages better than they spoke one but who still couldn't find work, about the other jobs they would do when they weren't driving, about how they hoped to visit America one day. And then when the heat succeeded in stupefying us beyond the possibility of conversation, I would read.

Before I left for Egypt, an English professor had given me a copy of an old *Granta*, a travel writing issue from the early eighties. Even now, over a decade later, I can remember the cover, soft on the corners, slightly tattered, and I can rattle off the names of the writers—Theroux, Chatwin, Thubron, Raban, Morris, and a handful of others. It's astonishing now to think they were all there, together, in one book. I treated the worn paperback as a map of sorts, not to any one place but rather to the kind of life I wanted for myself. I studied sections of it until whole passages were committed to memory. I must have read the book a half dozen times that year in the front seat of beat-up old taxis while they inched me across the Kasr al-Nil bridge, past the sooty stone lions that guard the entrance, and the opera house at the southern end of Gezira Island, around the massive traffic circle with the hulking government buildings. I would read a few lines and drift off to Siam, or Saigon, or Milan, only to be brought back to reality by the ear-splitting shriek of a horn or my driver's attempt to steal a few inches of open road from the car beside him. (Three years later, I watched thousands of ecstatic young Egyptians on TV march across the bridge and thought of how good it felt to come into the city dreaming.)

In my twenties, I went to Europe a few times as a tourist (though never, it seemed, to the right places). And I even lived in Japan for several years. Every time I'd get ready to leave home, my father would say, "Another big adventure." He meant it. He grew up in Kansas City and has spent most of his life in two states, logging hundreds of thousands of driving miles as a traveling salesman in the Midwest. To my father, a road trip to the Bootheel of Missoura is a tale worth telling.

"Another big adventure," he'd say. And I'd agree, even though it never really felt like a *real* adventure, a proper Shackleton-in-Antarctica, Burton-in-Africa, Thesiger-in-Arabia adventure. What it felt like was just moving my relatively predictable life from one side of the world to another while doing my best to dodge, delay, and altogether avoid growing up. And then, in the blink of an eye, as they say, I found myself settled in New York City at twenty-nine years old, where I spent the vast majority of my time either in an office or asleep. Dreams of a life spent wandering the world in the mold of my travel-writer heroes still taunted me, but now they did so from the past, rather than the future. On the road to adulthood, I'd somehow blown right past my turnoff. Hell, I hadn't even seen it go by.

Then, while I was visiting my sister in Seattle, something snapped. It was winter, and when the sun was high, the sky barely managed a soft pale gray. It rained constantly and everything iced over at night. It was absurdly melancholy, the "damp, drizzly

November" in Ishmael's soul that never failed to send the man to sea (albeit from the other side of the other country). I knew then that I couldn't spend another winter in New York, nor another summer. I'd had it. Some tiny thread—whatever was keeping me there—had been cut and all I could think about were the places I'd rather be: Tokyo, Lisbon, Berlin. Anywhere, really. I quit my job a week later, subleased my apartment, sold most of my stuff, and made arrangements to leave.

On my last night in the city, I took my dad, who had flown up to see me off, to a jazz club I liked, a basement room in the West Village. You had to drop a flight or two just to get inside. It was late and the band had already started by the time we got there. We took the only two open seats we could find, just to the right of the stage, which wasn't a stage at all, just the floor.

The band worked its way through a handful of songs, pushing and pulling the melodies, moving themselves from one end of the tune to the other as if on a tightrope. Good live jazz is surprisingly physical; the players wrestle with the music, toy with it, play it one way then another, size it up, look at it from a few angles. The band was great that night, but it's the drummer I remember. He was old, in his seventies at least, rail thin with light brown skin and deep creases in his face. He was a legend, actually; I knew his name from some records from the late 1950s. He'd played with everyone at one time or another. He wore elegant gray trousers and a striped button-down shirt, clothes that would have fit him when he was a little bigger. Now, they all hung loosely, making him appear like a dressed-up skeleton. But when he played, it was not hard to picture him in a room just like that one, fifty years younger.

His face flickered and flashed with expression, like he was watching a movie. His eyebrows lifted into question marks. He smiled when the pianist strung a few clever notes together. Every once in a while, he'd make himself laugh with something he did on the drums. The bandleader kept passing him solos and he'd take them, beat out a few bars on his own, and then count the band back in. The audience clapped. He smiled bashfully.

My dad and I were sitting on the wrong side of the lights, so the crowd was dark to us. The piano player was on the other side of the sax player, who had his back to us nearly the entire time. The only person we could see was the drummer, sweat pouring down his face, his body bent close to his kit like he might fold himself up into it. He played another solo, and another.

On the last song, the drummer really dug in. He played up and down the toms, called out on the snare, answered with a crash on the cymbals. The audience went quiet and he kept playing, alone. He played so lightly at one point, the drums whispered. We leaned in to listen. He played louder and faster until we were on the edges of our actual seats, thinking, *now maybe he should stop—he might give himself a heart attack.* The sweat around his collar bled dark in the spotlight. My dad leaned over and whispered in my ear: "He's going to kill himself doing that."

Finally, his face went calm; he cued the band. They came back in to roaring applause from a plainly stunned (and relieved) audience. But even as the song settled back into itself, it was clear the drummer was struggling. He took deep breaths, made nervous eye contact toward the back of the room. Someone said, somebody get him some water. We passed a glass up to him and set it down next to his hi-hat. Abruptly, he stopped playing. Standing up, he took a few weaving steps to the seat next to me and sat down, very still between breaths. Another drummer stepped in to continue the music. My drummer put his head in his hands. I could see his bony body under his shirt trying to fill itself with air. Another breath, slower this time. He grabbed his chest. I leaned over to him and asked if he was all right.

"Yes," he said, "I'm fine. It's just a heart thing." He smiled and looked at me through soft, yellow eyes. He said, "It's what I do."

He took a few sips of water, a few more deep breaths, and sat up straight. With a quick look to the sit-in drummer, he stood up gently. The audience erupted. He gave us an easy smile, sat down behind the drums, and picked up where he'd left off.

After the show, my dad and I climbed the stairs to the street where the cool air was waiting for us. It was a cold January night. I hailed a cab for him, and he gave me a hug. "Another big adventure," he said.

I started walking home—past Washington Square park, down Bowery, through Chinatown, and across the bridge. Anyone crossing the Brooklyn Bridge at night turns around to look at the city, and even though I'd seen it a hundred times, halfway across, I turned to see it again. But by the time I did, a curtain of clouds had fallen over Manhattan. The city twinkled and glowed silvery white from somewhere deep inside, but I felt stuck outside of it.

I turned back toward Brooklyn and, with an ache somewhere in my own chest, I walked until my feet hurt.

2

I flew to Japan the next day, landing at Narita on a clear afternoon. I like seeing big cities from the air. It's the only way to get a sense of their natural borders, the odd shapes they take. Even from the tallest buildings, it's hard to see the end of Tokyo. But from six and a half miles up, it's a scale model with a blue sea on one side and candy mountains on the other. It's dotted with bright green parks and covered in toy cars. Only from the sky can something so massive, sprawling, and complex seem so straightforward, so simple.

I had gone to be with my girlfriend, who had moved to Tokyo a year earlier because she hated New York and (I suspect) missed good soba noodles. We broke up almost immediately after I arrived, which felt inevitable as soon as it happened, and the weeks that followed exist in my memory as one long, gunmetal-gray afternoon. I wandered around the city visiting the perfectly manicured gardens and the temples swarming with tourists. I practiced my half-forgotten Japanese at Yoshinoya counters. I spent a lot of time alone in my hotel room reading Hemingway novels wishing I'd lived a century earlier and day-dreaming myself into heroic wartime fantasies. It was February and cold; short days without sunshine and long, looping walks to Harajuku, Omotesando, Asakusa, and back to my hotel. I exhausted myself tramping around the city. When it rained, I walked underground through the connected subway stations. I would leave my hotel, pick a direction, and walk until I was sure I'd pass out when I got back. In retrospect, it's pretty clear that I was moving in literal as well as metaphorical circles because I had no idea what I was supposed to do next. I couldn't go home; that would be too pathetic. I couldn't stay in Japan, because what would I do there? All I could do was walk, in circles. The soles of my feet still flinch when I think of Tokyo.

One night, a week and a half after arriving, I couldn't sleep. At a little past midnight, I got dressed and headed downstairs. The man at the front desk was asleep with his feet up and his hat over his eyes, the way doormen sleep in movies. I tiptoed outside. The street was ink-black except for the fluorescent glow of four or five vending machines. In front of one, a man in a suit had passed out and was lying curled up with his back toward the light, as if it might keep him warm. I jammed my hands in my pockets and made for the center of Shinjuku.

Not much was happening in the famed entertainment district other than a few people rubbing their eyes and chain-smoking cigarettes outside of a bar. A little pile of butts was collecting in a filthy heap in front of them. I kept walking. At some point the streets narrowed and the *yakitori* joints closed in on me, as if they were growing on top of one another. It was more crowded here, too, as if I'd wandered into some Miyazakian nightmare—not scary, exactly, but not quite right. Soon the walls closed in even more, and on either side of me shoebox bars were bursting with sweaty people drunkenly slurping and breathing and shouting. Faces slathered with the garish incandescence of a Bruce Gilden photograph streamed past me in a thousand different directions. From one bar came the canned music and sad, atonal warbling of a woman deep in the throes of karaoke, from another the guttural lowing of middle-aged men trying to speak through jaws and tongues made heavy from cheap sake. Shinjuku is not a large area, but it is, in places, devilishly convoluted, and it's possible to get very lost, as I did that night.

Ignoring my internal navigation, which was sending me in a feedback loop of weird dollhouse streets, I finally found my way out and onto a quiet and slightly larger street. In the middle of the road, two women were squatting and talking softly in the white circle of a streetlight, as if it were their living room. I stopped in front of a bar and puzzled over its name, which was spelled out in Katakana, the Japanese alphabet usually used for foreign words. I couldn't figure out what it was supposed to say. Often, these are English words written in Japanese as they would be pronounced by a Japanese person—*ko-hi* for coffee, *to-i-re* for toilet, and so on. If you're not that good at reading, which I'm not, it takes a bit of codebreaking. But the results are usually funny, or at least satisfying, like coming up with the right answer for a crossword clue. Intrigued, and tired of walking in circles, I went inside.

The interior was a rectangular space large enough for six people, with a long bar running down the center. Two salarymen sat at one end, drunk and swaying to the music like flaccid kelp leaves on the ocean floor. At the other end, two or three seats away from me, was a pretty woman with a round face lit up by the light of her phone. Behind the bar, a one-armed man sat on a low stool and kept his eyes trained firmly on the ground as if it might run out from under him. When I sat down, he cracked the top off a bottle of beer and set it in front of me. It was not hard to imagine some low-level yakuza killing a few hours here in the 1970s.

An easy silence, punctuated gently by some sad Lester Young tune, settled over the five of us. I asked the bartender what the name of the place meant. Without looking up he mumbled a response that I had no hope of understanding and said something to the girl, who broke from her phone to squint at me through bleary eyes.

"Where are you from?" she asked.

"America," I said. "New York."

Her name was Mari. She had been to America once, but only to "Disney." She worked here, in Shinjuku. Her job, she complained, involved too much drinking and too much talking. And too much singing. She said my Japanese was very good (it's not—I hadn't said more than ten words). She asked what I was doing in Tokyo, and I gave an answer that was probably too long and personal. She offered a sympathetic look in response. "Poor you," she said.

"I asked him what the name of the bar meant. It's in Katakana."

"Eh? It's in Katakana?" This was directed toward the bartender, who just grunted.

"Do you know what it means?"

"I've never thought about it."

"Is it Japanese?"

"Maybe," she said, typing something into her phone. Then she leaned over the barstools between us and showed me the screen, which showed Chinese characters and six English words: TOMORROW A NEW DAY THE SUN. She said, "It's something like this, an expression." She sat up in her chair and lifted her face to the ceiling. With both hands she traced an arc in the air and said in English, "Tomorrow za sahn," before sinking back into her phone for the rest of the night.

When I woke up late the next morning, my TV was on and a weather girl was chirping about the weather with a map of Europe in the background. Greece looked considerably warmer. Many degrees warmer, in fact. And sunny.

Landing in Athens was like disappearing. I didn't know a single person in the country, let alone the city. In fact, I could count my Europe-residing friends on one hand. I was thousands of miles away from anyone. And where Tokyo had held me at arm's length, Athens was wide open. Not just to me, but to everyone—immigrants fleeing war-torn countries, wealthy businessmen in expensive Italian suits, student anarchists throwing postapocalyptic parties outside my room (complete with barrel fires), and oblivious vacationers goose-stepping up to the Parthenon. We all shared the same smoggy Greek air, we all ate the same lukewarm gyros. I stayed for two weeks. I walked the city, drank bitter coffee, and read.

On a Monday, I left Athens on a bus for Monemvasia, a teardrop-shaped island off the coast of the Peloponnese and the site of a massive medieval fortress and several Byzantine churches. A man sitting next to me asked where I was going, and when I told him, he swooned. "Beautiful, beautiful Monemvasia," he said. Greeks have a remarkable ability to speak in travel-brochure quotes when discussing their country with foreigners, a cultural trait perhaps honed from centuries of showcasing their national treasures to the rest of the world like real estate agents with multimillion-dollar mansions.

"The most romantic place in all of Greece," he said.

"So I've read."

"But you came at the wrong time. You must come back in the summer! And you must visit the islands. Mykonos! Santorini! And you have a woman?"

When I told him that I couldn't come in the summer because I was already there and that I didn't have a woman, he immediately lost interest in me and spent the rest of the ride frowning at the back of the seat in front of him.

He was right, though. Monemvasia was romantic and beautiful. It was also completely dead, and the fortress was closed for repairs. So the following day, I headed for the Mani, a deeply weird finger of land in southwest Greece (supposedly) awash in old blood feuds and dotted with tiny clusters of stone tower houses. I had read a book about the Mani by Patrick Leigh Fermor in which he travels the country with a donkey and enjoys charming interactions with the locals. They take him in and perform traditional songs for him. He swims in what might be the portal to Hades. Already fluent in Greek, he delights in the nuances of the regional dialect.

My experience was different, though not entirely unpleasant, thanks to the pervasive otherworldliness of the place. A strip of mountains runs down the center of the peninsula and the whole thing gets bludgeoned with winds coming in off the sea. Parts of it could have stood for another planet in a science fiction movie. I went days without seeing a single person other than the old man who ran the hotel I was staying at, an exceedingly friendly Greek in his late sixties whose father had been friends with Leigh

Fermor but who himself had no memory of the man. Greece in the low season is pretty empty, but the Mani was desolate. Whole towns were entirely deserted. One morning, I walked to what I thought was the most southern point in continental Europe. I was wrong—it's in Spain, actually, at a place I had visited a few years earlier and forgotten about. Regardless, I felt like I had reached the end of the world, stepped outside of it. And now I had no choice but to turn around and go back in.

With spring finally breaking, I went north to Thessaloniki and then across the border into Macedonia. For the next four months, I bounced from one Balkan town to the next: tiny villages and empty seaside cities on the Albanian coast; odd little Austro-Hungarian hamlets with perfectly gridded streets (and very few people) in Montenegro; Ottoman enclaves in Bulgaria, Bosnia, and Kosovo. Plotted on a map, my route would resemble nothing so much as the excited doodles of a kindergartener. It was a great time, an aimless, exalting, exhausting, whale of a time. But by April I was running out of steam and money. What I needed was somewhere quiet, somewhere I could settle down for a week or two and plot my next move. Basically, I needed a place to stop and think.

On a tip from a Serb I'd met in a city on the Bosnian border, and guided by a hand-drawn map, I headed south from Sarajevo to a twelfth-century monastery in the hills of central Serbia. Getting there involved at least three buses and a seven-mile walk, making it something of a proper pilgrimage. The monastery was founded by a Medieval Serb king who abdicated and took monastic vows. Under his son, it grew to become the center of Serbian culture and spirituality for centuries. In its eight-hundred-year existence, it has survived raids by Turkish invaders, earthquakes, and fires, not to mention the ever-shifting and highly combustible recent politics of the region. Though no longer the powerhouse it once was, it remains an astonishingly beautiful place, a fortified temple with two white marble churches and a mesmerizing collection of Byzantine frescoes. It is now home to a handful of monks and a small guesthouse run by Marko, a recovering heroin addict from Belgrade.

I arrived around three in the afternoon and asked if I might be able stay for a while. For a daily rate yet to be determined, I was given a large room with a window, two twin beds, and a desk. From my window, I could see the outer stone walls of the compound and the top of the dome on the central basilica. Here, I thought, I could finally get some thinking done! There was no way the sheer sanctity of the place would *not* rub off on me. With the monks, and the church, and the quiet, I would be able to stop wandering, to set my life on its proper course.

Instead, I developed a routine that involved waking late and whiling away the day drinking bitter Turkish coffee with Marko, whose other main responsibility was caring for an elderly monk who had taken a vow of silence so long ago that no one there was sure when he'd spoken his last word. Not surprisingly, Marko loved to talk. He was in his late thirties and had lived all over Yugoslavia—Kotor, Sarajevo, Pristina, Zagreb—and in Prague for a year. He had studied to become a conductor but never managed to finish his degree since all of his money kept going to his drug habit. I liked Marko and like to think he enjoyed having me around. His stories skipped around chaotically, but I found that I could pay very little attention and still get the general gist of them. Everything was either "totally crazy" or "super," except for the monastery, which was, quite accurately I think, both totally crazy and super.

Over coffee on my first morning, I asked again how much it would cost for the room. Marko shrugged my question off and said he was still waiting to hear from the head monk, adding, cryptically, that "a deal may be arranged." The deal, it turned out, was that I would help out around the monastery, mostly in the kitchen washing dishes, in exchange for a very good rate and meals with the monks, who ate in silence. I gladly accepted, happy to have some work to distract me from all the thinking I wasn't actually doing but was constantly feeling guilty about.

A week and a half into my new life as a dishwasher for holy men, Ekonom, one of the monks, found me in the kitchen.

"Hey Johnny." He said this to me every time I saw him, in an accent so thick it sounded as if the words were being filtered through a mouthful of yogurt. A slight smile cracked through his wiry red beard.

"*Dobro jutro*," I said, exhausting my Serbian. Ekonom was not his real name. He was called this, it was explained to me, because he was in charge of the monastery's finances. Whenever I asked him exactly what he did, he just said "farmer."

"Today we go to hermitage?"

I had heard about the hermitage from nearly everyone at the monastery, though no one would tell me where it was or how to get there. It was, apparently, a secret I had to earn.

We drove for about fifteen minutes in the monastery car, a dark blue Skoda, listening to a CD of Serbian Orthodox chanting. Ekonom pulled over on the side of the road at a point marked by absolutely nothing and led me to an invisible break in the trees. Two makeshift walking sticks were leaning up against a tree. He handed me one, and we went into the woods. The path climbed steeply, and soon we were both leaning hard into our steps and taking deep breaths. At one point he bent over, pulled a tiny strawberry from a bush, and popped it in his mouth. "Good," he said. I ate one and said, "good." Those were the only two words we spoke on the way up.

We climbed uphill for what felt like several hours before reaching a rope bridge that looked like a set piece from an Indiana Jones movie. On the far side of the bridge, a flight of stairs led up to a long, narrow catwalk that was attached to the face of a cliff. At the end of the catwalk was one of the most bizarre things I've ever seen: an oblong stone structure three stories tall, built into the wall and resembling a giant beehive with a dozen tiny windows scattered across the front. It was impossible to tell what was holding it up, how it had been built, or what it was even made of. The only thing that was clear was that it had been there for a very long time, so long in fact that it looked as though it had grown organically out of the rock rather than been built into it.

Ekonom led us up the rest of the way. Inside the hive were three minuscule chambers stacked one atop the other and connected by handbuilt wooden ladders: on the first floor an empty room; on the second a kitchen; on the third a bed. In each room, one of the walls was just the crumbly cliff face.

The hermitage, Ekonom told me, had been used periodically for as long as the monastery, but no one was staying there at the time. Still, it was stocked with the essentials, and Ekonom wasted no time finding a jar of coffee grounds and a bottle of *rakia*, Serbian brandy. He fired up a tiny gas burner for the coffee.

Carrying four tiny cups on a tray, I followed my guide to a section of the catwalk that was covered with a roof and outfitted with windows, a makeshift sunroom perched on the face of a cliff. Before us unfurled miles of rolling hills in gorgeously rippled green rows, like shockwaves frozen in time. And between the rotting wooden slats that made up the floor, I could see clear down to the jagged rocks that would kill us when the whole thing collapsed.

"*Živeli*," he said, raising his glass. To life.

"*Živeli*," I said. We clinked glasses and drank in silence. Ekonom sat back in his chair with the blissed-out look of a slightly high garden gnome. I tried to stay as still as possible so as not to upset the decaying bridge that was keeping us alive.

After a few minutes, though, I started to feel something like what I imagined my friend was feeling. I'm not sure if it was the alcohol (which smelled suspiciously like the solution I had used a few days earlier to clean tape off the church floor), or the quiet, or a mesmerizing bird that was not so much flying but floating in the sky before us, but I let myself settle into a state of deep tranquility. Something close to total numbness. Suddenly, suspended there with my monk, everything was very peaceful. The hike had pretty thoroughly exhausted me, but what I felt wasn't tiredness. It was perfect emptiness. There was nothing to say, nothing to do. I had nowhere else to be. I knew my legs would hurt in the morning, but for the moment I couldn't even feel them.

I wanted to ask Ekonom about this feeling, whether he had it, too. If it had anything to do with why someone might give up the already austere life of a monk in the monastery to move up to the hermitage. I wondered, too, if anyone ever went mad alone up in that nest. When I asked one of the monks at the monastery about his decision to take monastic vows, he told me, "It's a very hard decision, but a very simple life." Simple, maybe, but certainly not easy. The monks kept insane hours. They woke at four a.m., ate two meals a day in silence and as quickly as possible, and spent the rest of their waking hours working to keep the monastery semifunctional.

Perhaps a lifetime spent repeating the same hard work every day could lead to a more powerful version of what I was feeling. Had I gotten a taste of the holy life just by walking up to the hermitage? God, was I having a spiritual epiphany?

It turned out I was not. I was just tired and overwhelmed and, more than anything, touched—by the kindness the monks had shown despite not knowing me at all, by Ekonom's simple gesture of leading me to the hermitage, by the warmth of the *rakia* that we shared. I was immensely happy, too, clear-headed, open minded, inspired, and filled with the feeling that I was on the edge of *something*, some crucial insight, some important discovery.

Of course, I didn't discover anything. You always wake up from this feeling as if from a dream that you never want to end, and it's all gone in an instant. Try as hard as you want; you can't get back inside. But even if a full-blown revelation eluded me, a small seed of an idea did not. It was there, at a remote hideaway somewhere in southern Serbia of all places, and in the company of an Orthodox monk of all people, that I started thinking of a walk, an extended walk, not a stroll around a city but a real trek, through woods, through hills, over mountains, far away from crowds of people and cars; something simple but not necessarily easy, something repetitive, and, most important, something long. Days long, weeks long, even—a proper adventure.

I would have liked to talk to Ekonom about this idea. It felt important. But I couldn't bring myself to break the silence. Instead, I looked over at him, let my eyelids droop a little, and spread my face into a dopey smile.

"Good?" he asked.

By the time we got back to the car, my feet were two pulsing bags of pain attached inconveniently to the ends of my legs. Slate-colored clouds were racing us back to the monastery.

Two busloads of Russian children were supposed to be coming for dinner, but by eight thirty p.m. they still hadn't arrived. With a terrifying clap of thunder, the sky opened. Lightning thrashed the surrounding hills and turned the night into a frighteningly realistic recreation of a storm straight out of the Old Testament. At nine p.m. sharp, the Russians arrived, a bolt of lightning turned the room blue, and the power abruptly went out. Vesna the cook sparked her lighter and held it up to her face. "Candles," she said.

We served by candlelight, the Russians ate by candlelight, and I washed dishes by candlelight. Everyone treated this as fairly normal, but the night had an undeniably medieval vibe to it. If the power never came back on, I suspect the monastery and the monks would carry on as they had for centuries.

The lights came back on around two in the morning. Restless and buzzing and no longer able to ignore the dull pain creeping up my legs, I tossed around my tiny bed. Finally I gave up trying to sleep and opened my laptop to discover a Wi-Fi signal (the password was another monastery secret I had to earn and the Internet connection was highly unreliable). I googled various permutations of the search terms "long," "mountains," "hard," and "walk" until an image caught my eye. The picture showed a map with a lake at the top and an ocean at the bottom and the word *ALPS* in between. Running through the center, irrespective of a clutch of brown-and-white peaks, was a thick red line. I stared at the map, as if I were eight years old again, until I was seeing a red line on the inside of my skull.

Three months later, I took my first real step into the mountains.

3

In reality, the red line is a brown line. It is made of dirt and rock and grass, and it's been trampled smooth into the ground by millions of feet over the years. It goes by many names, but my favorite is La Grande Traversée des Alpes (my least favorite, and the most common, is the GR5, or Grande Randonnée 5). It's nothing, really—a short leg of a much longer path that runs all the way from the Hook of Holland to the Mediterranean. It is one silk thread in a vast spider web of trails, walking routes, running paths, and climbing lines—many of which are named, graded, and maintained—that, as if by magic, only become visible once you know they exist. This network, which covers nearly all of Europe, improbably connects Portugal to Russia, Finland to Italy, and Spain to Slovenia, loosely, by way of thousands of miles of foot paths. Many of these routes, of course, have been used for centuries by travelers, merchants, pilgrims, exiles, and adventurers. Now, they are used primarily by hikers, either for a few hours of walking during the summer, or for months or years. There are maps that give precise walking times, and signs along the way to keep people from getting lost; there are places to sleep and eat and park your car. It's all very civilized. But even with the modern trimmings, they exist, to me, in a slightly different world, an older world—one without paved roads, train tracks, or airports. That's part of their charm. They do not always describe the fastest way from point A to point B, but a good way, which is different. They do not promise to get you from Brussels to Berlin in seven hours, but they will get you there, eventually, and if you make the journey, you will be happy to have done so. I didn't know any of this at the time, though, since I had never thought about it. I only knew my red line, which I could not get out of my head.

In the days and weeks after I found the map (or, perhaps, the map found me), the seed blossomed into a full-fledged idea that, in turn, quickly grew into an obsession. Somedays it was all I could think about. I would picture myself in the photographs I had seen on the Internet, images of ice-capped mountains, of endless fields of wildflowers, of warm dining rooms full of like-minded (if substantially older) people. I could see myself alone in a high meadow at night, flat on my back, my hands laced behind my head, the stars blindingly bright from millions of miles away. I felt in my legs the good, muscular burn of a hard day's walk, the satisfaction that comes from using your body as it was meant to be used. I dreamt, as one dreams of a long-lost love, of walking myself into the sea. It was only once I'd committed to the journey, once I'd bought the plane ticket and told everyone what I planned on doing, that I started to worry about it.

By ten o'clock on that first morning in the mountains, a fog had seeped out of the ground and obliterated everything that wasn't within arm's reach. Squinting, I could see five or ten feet ahead; anything beyond that dissolved into a milky white world that, for all I knew, went on for hundreds of miles. If I had been at the base of Mont Blanc, or a hundred feet from the sea, or ten steps from another human, I wouldn't have known it. My pace slowed. My steps grew delicate, as if I'd wandered into a minefield. I felt a familiar panic in my stomach. I thought, what if a bear has already caught my scent? I wondered, are there bears in the Alps? I tried to remember what I had read about bears, but my memory is terrible with those kinds of details. Either they were or were not animals to be aware of in this part of the world.

What I could recall was a story about a beast that had tormented some region in France (I couldn't remember which one) in the middle of the eighteenth century. Children and women had disappeared left and right from villages and were later found drained of blood and only partially eaten. This went on for years until someone finally shot and killed the animal, which turned out to be "the Napoleon Bonaparte of Wolves," according to Robert Louis Stevenson. (Wolves! That's what it was, not bears.) The Beast of Gévaudan, as it was known, gave birth to a multitude of persistent myths, superstitions, and theories, including one that involved vampires and another that attributed the killings to the work of a local psychopath who dressed up as a wolf. More recent theories suggest that it was the work of not one but three wolves, only two of which were definitively killed. That left a third whose ancestors might still be roaming these very hills. (Actually, the beast was in the region of Gévaudan, as the name suggests, some three hundred miles from where I was that day, but, I didn't know that at the time.) All this is to say that I couldn't be sure I *wasn't* in danger, either from bears or wolves, and that was more than enough to make me reconsider the entire project for the hundredth time that week. Constantly reconvincing myself that what I was doing was not a terrible idea had become mentally exhausting, and that was on top of the actual physical exhaustion—the morning, my first, had been a humbling series of steep climbs that no amount of half-assed training (the only kind of training I did) could have prepared me for.

Still in the cloud, I stopped moving, unclipped and offloaded my pack for the first time that day, and leaned against a tree. My shoulders burned in a way that was a little alarming. My legs felt so tight I was afraid to sit down for fear that they would lock up like drying cement. I started moving again, in a small orbit around my tree, with my hands on my hips and my face scrunched in a sour little squint to keep the sweat out of my eyes. I kicked my legs back every few steps like a dog trying to cover its shit with grass.

The morning sky had been so clear and sharp it could have cracked like a frozen pane of glass if some poor bird had flown into it. Not an hour earlier, I was craning my neck to marvel at it through the treetops. Rain was one of the (many) variables I worried about most, so I was thrilled to have lucked into such fine walking weather on day one. The thought of having to trudge through a downpour always made me think of sopping wet soldiers in war movies with trench foot and pneumonia. God, I thought, that would be miserable. Nearly every person who knew of my plan asked what I would do if it rained. "Walk," I'd say. "What else?" In truth, I was sure I wouldn't walk in the rain. Plus, I harbored a warm, almost mystical, feeling that, against all meteorological evidence, I would enjoy an unprecedented string of dry, sunny days.

But I hadn't considered fog. I hadn't given a single thought to what it would be like to be completely alone in the mountains in an absolute whiteout. One discovers a whole new level of solitude on the inside of a cloud five thousand miles from home (and surrounded by an imaginary pack of human-eating wolves). One might even start talking to oneself in such a surreal moment. He might ask himself: "What am I doing here?"

With my phone, I took a blurry photograph of the fog. It's one of the earliest images I have of the walk, and naturally, it's essentially a photograph of nothing—just a hazy, wet whiteness. There are no details to pick out, nothing to show the scale or to mark the location. A person looking at it would assume it was a mistake, that I had my finger over the lens or that the shutter opened in my pocket. But I took it, and I didn't delete it then—though the thought crossed my mind—and I haven't deleted it since because the timestamp and GPS tag buried in the metadata is of sentimental value to me. The photo tells a story: I was in this place, at this time, and this is what I saw. I have the picture to prove it.

I took stock, put my thoughts in order. This is what I knew: the exact location of my next two footsteps, the sound of my blood pumping behind my ears, and the unbelievable weight of a thirty-pound backpack constantly pulling me toward the earth. According to my calculations, I should have already been about halfway to where I needed to be for the night—a *refuge* (a basic, staffed hut) just on the other side of the Swiss border. What I did not know (and what would have been helpful) was precisely where I was. I dug a map out of my bag and found Lake Geneva easily. Beyond that, it was impossible to say with any certainty where in relation to the lake I stood. I turned the map sideways, checked for topographical features I might recognize. Nothing. I was surrounded by trees, but there were trees from the Pyrenees to Vladivostok. Most of Europe was trees. Trees were useless.

I shouldered my pack and continued south. Always go south, I thought. The going was tough, very tough, but nothing like it had been earlier in the day. This was actually manageable. And despite the persistent doubts, I felt pretty good. I was even getting used to walking with poles so I might not have looked like a newborn deer tottering on four stick-thin legs.

Then the path dead-ended abruptly at a fence made of two horizontal strands of twine. This was surprising, to the say the least. But more befuddling was a small yellow sign hanging from the fence with an illustration of a black hand shooting lightning bolts out of it. *ELECTRIQUE*, it added fancifully. I could see the trail stretching out ahead on the other side. I looked at the sign for a long time, the way someone might look at their dog if it started talking. Was I lost? It was possible, but unlikely. Getting lost was something else I worried about, so I had been very careful not to stray from the path. Maybe the fence wasn't actually electrified, or maybe the sign was just a deterrent. A deterrent against what though? Animals escaping? That didn't make any sense. Maybe the sign was to keep people like me out, lost people, silly Americans with grand plans of walking across mountains. I thought about testing the fence by throwing one of my walking poles at it, but I was soaked in sweat and the air was all moisture. With my luck, the whole forest would go up in a white-hot cloud of electricity.

No, I thought, the sign was a sign—the universe's way of making very clear what should have been obvious from the start: walking across the Alps was a bad idea.

The lightness of this realization was immediately relaxing. I had tried—that was undeniable. I'd given it my best shot and come up against a literal wall (well, fence). There was nothing left but to turn back. I could be back in town by dinner, in Geneva the next day. I'll take a train to Berlin, find an apartment, get a job, forget this whole thing.

I was still looking at the sign with a dumb grimace on my face when I heard the rapid approach of crunching branches behind me. For a split second, I was sure it was the wolf. How perfect: just when I'm about to throw in the towel, I get eaten by a wolf. I turned to face the beast. But what emerged from the fog was not an animal; it was a man, late-forties, wearing a baseball hat and bright yellow shoes. He moved very quickly, but his upper body remained perfectly level.

"*Bonjour*," he said, as he grabbed a rubber handle on the fence and unlatched the twine.

Dumbfounded, I managed to let out a soft *hello*. He stepped carefully over the bottom line, hooked the handle back up, and disappeared into the cloud until all I could see were the little yellow spots of his shoes bouncing out of view. His legs had never stopped moving even as he worked the latch, his feet rising and falling in short, vertical pumps. He had appeared and disappeared so quickly that I couldn't be sure I didn't imagine him. He may have been an angel sent to show me the way. And how had I not seen that handle? I chided myself for not paying close enough attention to anything, for worrying too much, for seeing cosmic signs where there weren't any, for feeling so relieved to turn back. Deflated, I opened the gate and stepped gingerly over the wire, careful not to electrocute myself.

Forty-five minutes later, the trees thinned out and the earth leveled off completely. The fog had weakened slightly, too, and I could see fifteen or twenty feet in every direction. I stood on the edge of what looked like large field and followed the path with my eyes until it broke up in a patch of churned mud. The sky was gone. Just the faintest glow of the sun remained, round and white, above me. The only thing I could see was the earth around, green and brown grass slicked and softened from days of rain and the heavy movements of large animals.

A breeze kicked up and the cloud swirled. Small windows opened in the fog ahead, and I followed the gaps into the clearing, the flat ground a welcome gift after so many hours of climbing. I'd been walking for five hours at that point, mostly uphill on soft muddy ground that had sent me slipping backwards every few minutes. I followed the path in my small bubble of visibility. It was like being in a deep-sea vessel on the ocean floor. At a glistening clump of white boulders, I worked at dislodging myself from my pack until it dropped with a *thunk* and bounced a little down a small hill. I felt instantly and immeasurably lighter. Then wobbly all of a sudden, out of balance, and dizzy. Hunger, I thought. In fact, I was starving since I hadn't eaten anything that day except a cup of tepid coffee. I had six energy bars and a jar of peanut butter with me, which I considered emergency rations. In a pinch, I figured I could survive on them for a night or two. What had I planned on eating for lunch? Good question.

I tore into the energy bars and, sinking to the ground with my legs sticking straight out in front of me like a confused grizzly bear, ate three in quick succession. Then I ate one more. I noticed then, for the first time, the way my body was only able to handle one problem at a time. Once I realized how hungry I was, I completely forgot about the pain in my feet and legs. This automatic prioritizing became apparent at other times, too. If I was climbing up a steep hill, I only felt my legs burning. If I walked downhill, my knees ached like an old man's, but my legs felt strong. If I was hot, I dreamt of getting cool. Only the most immediate physical issue occupied my attention. I came to enjoy this, marveling at my natural ability to compartmentalize pain and suffering.

The energy bars helped immediately, something else that fascinated me then and would continue to astonish me for weeks to come: despite twenty-nine years of doing it wrong, my body could still use food efficiently. It knew how to convert carbohydrates, proteins, and fats to energy, and if I ate right and often enough, I would experience only brief lulls in energy. (A man I met much later who walked with a pedometer told me he burned, on average, between five and six thousand calories a day. I have no idea if this is accurate, but there is no question that my daily expenditure of energy was considerable. Within a week I would eat whatever food I could find since I knew I would still feel hungry a few hours later. In the spirit of adventure, I figured, I would learn by making mistakes. Loads of them.)

The ground beneath me was so soft that if I lay down, I was sure I would fall asleep. I closed my eyes and took deep breaths until the sound of my own breathing was the only thing I could hear. The pumping blood quieted. A high-pitch ringing softened until it faded out completely. My legs went numb. A silent, narcotic exhaustion came over me, and I let myself go under.

4

By that point, I hadn't slept well in so many days that I wasn't sure how long it had been. I would guess the last good night of sleep had come five days earlier, in my old bedroom on the second floor of my parents' house.

That Sunday (or was it Monday?), I had taken a seven a.m. flight from Kansas City to Newark. I sat next to a man whose only carry-on was a Macy's shopping bag full of newspapers. From taxi to touchdown, he spread, folded, unfolded, respread, rotated, and refolded the papers in what could only have been practice for the world's worst sleight-of-hand trick. His fingers smudged the ink until they were black with it.

For airplane- and soon-to-be-walking reading, I had chosen, in an especially ambitious mood at the last second, *War and Peace*. I knew from the jacket copy that it had something to do with Napoleon's invasion of Russia and was thus not unrelated to

France, which, my thinking went, made it perfect reading for a walk through the Alps. Plus, it would easily be the longest book I had read on the longest walk I had walked, a feat within a feat. I opened to page one—an introduction. I never know what to do with introductions, and usually skip them, but given the length of this trip, I figured I would need every word I could get. By the end of the first paragraph, in which the author offers a fair warning to the reader that the book is "as vast as Russia and as long to cross from one end to the other," my mind was drifting off to a long-standing dream I have of crossing Russia on foot from one end to the other. Maybe I should save this book for that trip, I thought. I peeked ahead to see how long the introduction went on. Thirty pages, followed by another lengthy section on the principal characters. I skipped to page one proper, which is in French, a language I can't read.

I stuck with it, though, digging deep to recall a semester of French I had taken in college. But every few minutes the corner of a rogue broadsheet from the man next to me would find its way on top of my book or in front of my face or in my ear, break my concentration, and make it impossible to conjugate even the most basic verbs. The effort alone lulled me half to sleep. Russia would have to wait for France.

I closed the book, then I closed my eyes. But sleep wouldn't come. In fact, as soon as my eyes were shut, I felt even more awake. I opened them again and let the drowsiness pull my eyelids down, and the pattern repeated itself. Without fail, just when I would nod off, my brain would rally like I was driving on a highway at three a.m. After an hour of this, I couldn't tell if I was having a nightmare about constantly being woken up on the verge of sleep or if my brain was torturing me like some black-site interrogator. Between the newspaper folding and my slow-motion bobblehead, the two of us almost certainly looked insane. One of us might have been.

At Newark with a four-hour layover, I did dozens of laps around the terminal to ensure complete exhaustion for the upcoming transatlantic leg. My pace alternated between a slow shuffle and a nervous speed walk. The thought of an eight-hour flight trapped in sleep limbo was making me anxious. I didn't sit down until I was back on a plane (the last plane, in fact, that I would be on for a very long time).

The plan was simple: I would arrive in Geneva at seven in the morning (midnight in Kansas City), and spend the day buying a few supplies. The following day I would catch a bus to a small town across the French border, at which point I'd start walking. When I got tired, I would find a place to stop for the night. Admittedly, these were not the best laid plans; they were barely plans at all, really. More like rough sketches of thin outlines of plans.

What happened was this: I did not sleep on the overnight flight. I sat awake, just barely. I teetered frustratingly on the edge of somnolence all the way across the Atlantic and halfway across Europe. I watched on a small screen as the plane traced its graceful arc over the ocean and across northern, then central, France. The little airplane icon ticked right, one pixel at a time, so slowly it might as well not have moved at all. I thought about how badly I needed to sleep, which made it worse. All I wanted to do was close my eyes and wake up when the wheels touched the ground. I shivered in the air-conditioning, then sweated when it cycled off. Anyone watching me would have thought I was sick with some terrible fever. And maybe I was. I tried Tolstoy again with even less success than before.

I don't remember landing, or collecting my baggage, or getting to my hotel. I have clearer memories of life as an infant than

I do of the twenty-four hours I spent in Geneva. It is a testament to Swiss efficiency that I managed to do anything at all in such a fried state of mind. But I did. In fact, I got up to all sorts of things. I know I bought walking poles, because I had entered Europe without them, and I have them now. But I could not say where I got them or how much I paid. I believe I took a bus or a train into the city since I have a stub, but the words don't ring any bells. And I know I walked around the city center because when I look at images of the city today, certain places look familiar, like scenes from a movie I haven't seen in years. I have exactly one note in my journal about that day: "Ate lunch at lunch." Geneva is the only city I can say I've been to in what amounts to a near-total blackout.

And then another night without sleep: the hard slap of rain falling in sheets against a window in perfect three-second intervals; the click-rev-hum of an air-conditioner turning on and off and on and off; the relentless tapping of drops on the roof. Footsteps down the hall. The loud, irregular thump of my own heart. These are the sounds, I was sure, that roar like a jet engine inside an insomniac's head as he's losing his grip on reality. It was all mixed, that night, in a soup of anxiety, jet-lag, and the occasional burst of adrenaline. In the darkness, I reached for my phone, stopping just short. Don't give up, I thought. Keep trying. Sleep will come. Sleep will come. Sleep will come. But as soon as I hit the home button a warm feeling spread through me like a shot of whiskey.

I scrolled through Twitter like I might get to the end of it, checked my email, and texted my brother in New York.

"Hey."

"Hey."

"Can't sleep."

"What time is it there?"

"No idea."

"Try not holding an iPhone screen four inches from your face."

But it was too late; the light from the screen had blasted my brain back to full wakefulness. I googled Geneva and learned, apropos of nothing, that the city's name probably comes from the Celtic word for *bend*, as in a bend in the river. It shares this etymological note with Genoa, Italy (Genova in Italian). This is perhaps the least interesting fact about either Geneva or Genoa, cities that have been at the center of European history for centuries. But at three a.m., I loved the obvious-once-you-know-it quality of the information. How many thousands of cities and villages in the world are named "bend"?

I wondered if it was the same river that bends in both Geneva and Genoa. Hadn't I been reading about Genoa somewhere? *War and Peace*! I opened the first page, and there it was, the very first sentence: "*Eh bien, mon prince, Gênes et Lucques ne sont plus que des apanages, des estates, de la famille Buonaparte.*" I followed a footnote to learn that, in 1797, Napoleon had made Genoa into a French protectorate and then annexed it in 1805. From Geneva to Genoa. God, I thought, *that* would make a great title. I looked for Genoa on a map. It was certainly in the right direction (south), but I would have to reroute significantly. Still, it could be done.

It was at that point that I realized I was truly losing it. I would not be rerouting to Genoa simply because it shared a linguistic thread with Geneva. I would not be going to Genoa because Tolstoy had mentioned it in the first line of *War and Peace*. More immediately, I would not be going to Genoa because I would not be going anywhere if I didn't get some sleep.

(Deeper down the rabbit hole that night, I learned that Kansas City, my hometown, got its name from rivers and from the French language. It was the French explorer Etienne de Bourgmont who, while exploring the Missouri River, first rendered the name of the Kansa River as *Cansez*, a reference to the Kansa people who inhabited the region. And it was, of course, Napoleon who sold French Louisiana, which included what is now Kansas City, to the United States in 1803. My brain, fumbling in the dark, was busy drawing all kinds of flimsy connections.)

I tapped the weather app without thinking, which was a mistake. The next nine days on the calendar showed images of little rain clouds and the background of my screen was a burbling black cloud that spit lightning bolts to the edges of my phone. The effect in that moment was utterly deflating, like waking up from a particularly real dream about winning the lottery. The only silver lining I could find on these clouds was the chance that I had reached the nadir of a very real nightmare—and all I had to do was wake up, which I would do any minute now.

In the morning, I dragged myself through the rain to a bus station that looked more like a junkyard and was squeezed into the parking lot of a church in what appeared to be one of Geneva's more industrial neighborhoods. In preparation for the hours of walking I still planned on doing that day, I was dressed as a full-on outdoorsman: heavy rubber boots, quick-drying trousers, shirts, and jumper in various shades of green, as well as a bulging backpack and gleaming walking poles. A group of what I took to be passengers huddled under an awning while a sopping homeless man politely approached each person and asked for money. He had a few patchy bags that were ingeniously attached to his body with ropes and bungees. If I had given him one of my poles, we would have cut strikingly similar figures. I sidled up to the group as inconspicuously as I could.

I wanted to get there early to buy a ticket, but the ticket office was closed and wouldn't be open until well after my bus was scheduled to leave. Scanning the group for a sympathetic face, I found one on a girl about my age.

"I'm sorry," I said to her, preemptively apologizing for whatever stupid words were about to come out of my mouth. "Do you know if I can buy a ticket on the bus? I'm trying to get to Thonon." I pronounced *Thonon* with an emphasis on the second syllable.

"Thonon?" she repeated back to me in a way that sounded exactly like what I had said.

"Thonon?" I tried, shifting the weight to the first syllable.

"It is a city?"

"I think so. In France, maybe an hour from here. The bus is supposed to leave soon."

"Ah, Thonon!" To my ears, her pronunciation sounded just like mine. "I am going there, too," she said. "Yes, you can buy a ticket on the bus."

Smiling at her like a fool, I struggled to think of something else to say and only managed a *cool* after a long a pause.

The bus arrived an hour late, and—with the ticket booth still not open—I stepped aboard with cash in my hand like a teenager about to buy some beer. "Thonon," I said as I handed him a twenty-franc note, the smallest I had. From the look of disgust on the man's face, you'd be forgiven for thinking I had handed him a dead animal. There followed a torrent of plosive French while the man rummaged through half a dozen bins and wallets to make up the change. Eventually he gave up, put my twenty back in my hand, and sent me to the back of the bus with a jerk of his thumb. My bag, with its straps, poles, and dangling sneakers, snagged on every seat along the way. But two hours later (three hours late, if we're keeping track), I stepped off the bus and breathed a great sigh of relief upon the realization that, for the next four hundred miles, I would not have to deal with another angry French bus driver.

Thonon-les-Bains sits on the south shore of Lake Geneva. It has a lovely main square lined with cafés that, in the rain, gave it a moody, introspective sheen. It is one of two semiofficial starting points for the *Grande Traversée.* There are actually a handful of starting routes from the lake up into the mountains, but I chose Thonon as my departure point because I needed to make a decision, and it seemed as reasonable a place as any other.

The rain, which had slowed to a drip, finally stopped. I sat on a bench, pulled a small map from my bag, and set about figuring out which way to go. The map, of course, was far too small and, no matter how hard I stared at it, revealed nothing beyond the fact that the lake was north and I needed to go south.

A voice: "*Pardon,* can I help?" It was the girl from earlier, standing over me like an angel. Even though we had not spoken more than fifteen words to each other, and I didn't know her name, I can't describe how good it felt to see her at that moment. Sadly, she was the closest thing I had to a friend in all of France. I explained that I was trying to find the trail that would leave the town toward Chevenoz.

"You cannot do this today. It's too late." It was one o'clock.

"Are you sure? It doesn't seem that far."

"Yes, I have walked this many times. You will not make it before night and anyway the weather is very bad."

"Well, is there somewhere I can stay between here and there? Even if it's only a couple hours of walking, I'm anxious to start moving today."

"No, I don't think so. You should stay in Thonon and leave in the morning. Tomorrow the sun will be out," she said in a weird echo of something I'd heard before. "There are many nice hotels in town. My boyfriend's father has a hotel not far from here. I can give you the address." She typed the address in my phone and walked away, leaving me on a wet bench clutching my phone in one hand and a crumpled, useless map in the other.

I considered the possibility of going to St. Gingolph, another recognized starting point a little farther east, but as far as I could tell the only bus going that way left too late in the day to make any difference. There was a bus leaving in an hour to La Chapelle d'Abondance, the mountain town where, according to a guide book I had (Paddy Dillon's compact and invaluable *The GR5 Trail*, henceforth called *the book*), I was to sleep the next night. This meant, essentially, not only skipping two days of walking, but skipping the first two days of walking by paying for a bus. It would be like cycling the first mile of a marathon and running the rest; you're still doing twenty-six miles, but no one cares. Watching pigeons jump around the square, I thought about what that would mean for the integrity of my walk, how pathetic it would be, how typical, really. I thought about it until the bus pulled up, and then I thought about it more as I took my seat even as the bus wound its way slowly up the wet mountain roads. It was a shameful decision, the first failure in a long string of them in my botched start. But, as I saw it, I had no real choice. I was terrified of spending another sleepless night doubting the trip. At least now I had started, no matter that I had cheated. I told myself—promised—I would go back and walk the first two days once I had finished.

La Chapelle d'Abondance is everything one could want for one's first French mountain town. It is tiny, secluded, and old—an assemblage of adorable chalets and traditional farmhouses clustered in a verdant valley below eight-thousand foot peaks. There is, as there should be, a church—The Church of St. Maurice—topped with a bell tower of two copper balls, a boulangerie, a fromagerie, and a handful of other shops and restaurants.

The first hotel I tried was full, which was not a good sign. In the spirit of adventure and against the advice of several sources, I hadn't made any sleeping arrangements along the way. Doing so would have required far too much research; however, more than that, I was afraid I would uncover some incontrovertible reason for not going. I didn't want to find out, for example, that everything was booked for the next three weeks, or that someone had just died en route, or, worse, that another twenty-nine-year-old American was planning the same trip. Everyone back home knows the Appalachian Trail, the Pacific Crest Trail, the John Muir Trail. But so few seem to have heard of the Grand Traverse of the Alps. English-language information on the Internet was scant, limited to a couple of websites and daily logs on hiking boards. There was something untouched about it that I liked, so I treated it preciously, like a secret.

The second hotel I tried had a room free, which meant all was not lost. As I was checking in, the girl showing me my room asked where I had come from, and I lied for the first of many times. "From between Thonon and here," I said. She was just making conversation, but I felt my face burn with shame as soon as I said it, and I suspect she saw right through me. "We are having a dinner with the guests at seven. You are welcome to join. As you like."

I dropped my bag in the room and went out for a walk. Rain drizzled slow and steady as if the clouds were trying to make it last. It looked like it might go on forever. In a café, I drank a beer and watched a man covered head to toe in blue Gore-Tex slowly pull himself across the village with his walking poles. He walked with such calm, such authority. He did not look nervous or bothered by the conditions; he simply sliced through the elements. The rain hit him and rolled off in a million tiny beads. I sipped my beer until it was gone and asked for another.

At dinner I lied again, this time to an audience of lovely Dutch people who deserved better. Through my teeth, I told a group of middle-aged men and women sipping French wine and popping slices of cheeses in their mouths that I had walked from Thonon and would go to Nice. Not only did they doubt my story, but also my sanity. Did I know about mountains? Did I have the right equipment? Was I conditioned? Naturally, my answers failed to convince anyone, least of all myself, of the feasibility of the project. And having hit an investigative dead end, the table tilted back into Dutch while I silently reprimanded myself for being such an ass. A few more glasses of wine and my head sloshed with self-pity. Would it have killed me to say I had taken a bus here because of the rain? That I was operating on only a few hours of sleep over the last few days? That I had no idea what I was doing? That I wished more than anything to wake up in my own bed in Kansas, the flattest, safest place in the world?

Back in my room, the world was liquid. Half awake, I floated on my bed to the sounds of people laughing and clinking glasses down the hall while the rain beat a white noise on the window.

I closed my eyes and pictured an ocean of warm water underneath the ground, rising and falling. I felt the swell build gently beneath me, push me up and carry me down. A Conrad quote I had read somewhere floated into my head—something about a man falling into the sea and drowning when he tries to get out. For the life of me I couldn't put the words in the right order or remember the line, but I felt very much like a man who had fallen into the sea, like a man trying to climb out.

I lay flat on my back until the alcohol wore off and things grew less rubbery. At two a.m., I tried Tolstoy again. (At 2:15, I gave up). By three, a headache had crept in behind my eyes. On the nightstand, I found a brochure touting all the activities one can find in the Vallée d'Abondance. It was filled with pictures of families looking genuinely happy while doing dangerous things: families running down mountains, families kayaking, and families rock climbing. One photo showed an elderly couple, silver haired and effortlessly fit, hiking through a green pasture that exploded with wildflowers. The caption read *randonnée*. Hiking. They made it look so simple, these people! Why was I making it look so hard? I ran through all the answers until, around four a.m., my eyes finally closed and my brain clicked off.

The electric chime on my phone jerked my eyes open an hour and forty-five minutes later. My arms and legs were lead. In that short time, I had achieved a sleep so deep that I could have gone back under and stayed there for a week. Instead, I fought like a man in quicksand until I could sit up on the edge of the bed, where I stayed for a long while. I got dressed, shouldered my bag, took a deep breath, and slipped outside the back of the hotel.

Sunrise was still at least an hour away, and I debated whether or not I should wait a bit to leave. I had a headlamp and desperately wanted to get moving, but the town was black. Clouds blocked the moon and stars. I stood there, locked with indecision.

"*Bonjour,*" a man said behind me, scaring me half to death.

He had a mess of white hair and looked identical to one of the healthy people from the brochure. He lit a cigarette, offered me one, and asked where I was headed. I said to Nice, and he laughed. "No," he said, "for tonight."

"Chesery. In Switzerland."

"It's beautiful there. Wild."

I asked if it was a long way and he said it was a good day's walk, but not too bad. It was my first day walking, I explained. His eyes narrowed as he exhaled the smoke.

"*Café?*" he asked. He disappeared back inside and came back a minute later with two small cups of black coffee that we drank standing up. To the east, the sun started to brighten the sky.

"These mountains are special, you know. There is no place in the world like the Alps. We come every year from Belgium to spend time here," he said. We finished our coffee without another word, the two of us gazing pensively into the distance. Then he slipped back inside and left me to take my first steps into the mountains alone.

5

Dreaming of warm sand and cool water, I sank deeper into the soft ground. The sleep that had been cut short by my phone that morning greedily sucked me back under. I lay on the ground, perfectly still. I couldn't have moved even if I wanted to. It occurred to me—for the first time—that no one, including myself, knew where I was. Other than the running man, I hadn't seen another person for hours, not since I left La Chapelle d'Abondance. I watched the mist swirl and move in patterns. I still couldn't see through it but followed its movement, the way a tail of smoke would curl until it dissolved. There were lovely subtleties in the color, too, once I really looked at it: rain-green here, pinkish-white there, the light playing gracefully off the grass, the rocks, the mountains. When a human head appeared above me, it was the most normal thing in the world. It's remarkable how real dreams can feel even when you know you are in one. This sensation is only amplified when you haven't slept in days.

"Are you okay?" the head said.

I stood up on shaky legs. "Yeah. Just resting."

"You were asleep."

"I'm tired. Where are you coming from?"

"Chesery."

"No, I mean where did you start walking?"

"The sea."

"The sea," I said, letting the word float out of my mouth. "Is it far?"

"*Oui*, it's far. But it's a good walk. You are coming from Léman?"

"From La Chapelle, actually."

"Ah, you start as I finish. Good luck!" He dug his walking sticks into the ground and took off, like a skier. Within ten seconds, I couldn't see him.

I walked into Switzerland a few hours later with all the fanfare of crossing the state line from Kansas into Missouri. If the frontier was marked, I didn't see it. There was no guard, no WELCOME TO SWITZERLAND sign. Nothing. There weren't any people around, either. Still, in my shaky, sleep-deprived, exhausted mind, I liked the idea of being (back) in Switzerland. It is not often anymore that a traveler has the chance to walk out of one country and into another—it was a first for me—and it's probably even less common to do so alone. It was the quietest of trespasses. No one knew and no one cared. But I'd crossed a border on the power of my own legs, and in a muted way, it was absolutely thrilling. Human history is full of migration, and for the overwhelming majority of our time on this planet, we've been hopelessly foot-bound. In a tiny, irrelevant way, I joined a long line of frontier-crossers that goes back to the beginning of the human race.

Well, at least I hoped I had crossed the frontier. According to a note I had, Switzerland lay on the other side of the final ascent of the day, and as far as I could tell I had crested it. (If I hadn't, I thought—if there was still more to climb—I might not make it. The hills earlier that day had been terribly punishing and my legs were dangerously unequipped for even the slightest incline. I can say without any doubt that, up to that point in my life, I had never felt as physically wrecked as I did climbing the last few feet of that last hill.)

The fog had burned off around lunchtime and through a layer of high, thin clouds, the sun drilled down all afternoon as if through a magnifying glass. Several people had warned me that the sun was more intense at higher altitudes. I carried only a small tube of sun screen, which I didn't want to rummage around my bag to find. What was at first rejuvenating, after such a wet morning, was now more than a little unnerving as my skin burned.

That last ascent of the day was nothing but a molehill, but I had to practically drag myself over it, stopping every few feet to sip water and rest. I reminded myself (somewhat flatteringly) of Thesiger crawling across the desert looking for water, on the verge of death. But Thesiger I was not. With any luck, dinner and a bed were waiting for me an hour away. I have no doubt the man would have laughed at my softness.

Unfortunately, Switzerland was just as miserably hot as France, and I still had an hour or so to go before reaching the refuge. I suffered on, stopping every few minutes to get my bottle from my pack and sip some water, which was running low. Eventually, I could just make out the building in the distance.

Energized at the thought of not having to take another step that day, I picked up the pace. Soon, the refuge and its surroundings revealed themselves. The main building, a stone cabin, was set on the edge of a small lake and surrounded on three sides by tall, grassy slopes. It was laughably remote and stunningly picturesque. I had never seen a place so isolated. There were no roads or cars. A narrow trail (the same one I was walking in on) snaked out and continued on over the slope to the south. The glassy lake reflected the bright green of the hills and gave the landscape a brilliant emerald glow. I might as well have walked into Oz.

I was two minutes away from a bench that was calling my name when a helicopter flung itself over the hill like they do in action movies and swooped down over the lake, where it hovered fifty feet up. The sound was deafening, as if someone had just flipped the switch on an airplane engine next to my head. A man in a yellow jumpsuit dropped a rope and followed it down with some kind of harness. From where I was standing, I couldn't see the action on the land, but in less than a minute a body was being hauled up into the chopper. With the rope and the jumpsuited man back inside, it banked and took off over the hill. The evacuation had lasted three minutes, tops. When the noise was gone, it was like it had never been there.

Inside the refuge, I asked about a bed and was told that they only had two people staying for the night. The room slept sixteen. A girl, Marie, led me back to the sleeping quarters, which was just a closet with two bunks running the length of the room, each one capable of holding eight bodies. I took a spot next to the wall in the far back corner.

"The shower is in the hall, and it has hot water. Dinner is at seven," she told me.

I thanked her and explained that it was my first time in a refuge. I wondered if there was some hut etiquette I should know about.

"Nothing special, she said. "Just take your boots off inside."

"Seems simple enough," I said. "So, do you live here?"

"No, just for the summer. I'm a college student, but my village is only about two hours away."

"By car?"

"No," she laughed. "Walking. I come at the start of the season and stay until the end. It's very quiet and a little boring, but I like it here. It's beautiful."

"I've never seen any place like it, actually."

"You are from England?"

"I'm American. I've been living in New York for the past few years."

"It is my dream to visit New York. But I think it's too many people."

"Well, compared to this, a full car is too many people." It was a stupid thing to say, but she laughed, anyway.

"Do you want some tea?"

I took my tea outside and sat at a table across from a stocky man in his mid-forties named Bernard. Bernard was from Paris and had also walked that day from La Chapelle d'Abondance. But where I looked like I'd been chased by a pack of wild dogs, Bernard looked like he could have flown in on the helicopter. He smiled over a stack of maps and, every few seconds, chucked an almond in his mouth. He told me he was going all the way to Nice and planned to do it in twenty-six days. By his count, that left no rest days and no buffer days for bad weather. If it rained, he would walk in the rain. If it snowed, he would walk in the snow. He had already booked accommodation for the next twenty-five nights and delaying even one day would mean a nightmare of rescheduling. When I asked why he had locked himself into such a punishing schedule, he said he had to be back at work. This was his vacation. He popped another almond in his mouth.

"And you? You will go to Nice?"

"That's my plan, but I'm in no rush, so I don't know how long it will take me. I've never really done any hiking before."

He stopped chewing. "In France?"

"Anywhere."

"You have not walked in mountains before this?"

"No. Today was my first day." I gave a confusing explanation of why I had started in La Chapelle rather than at Lake Geneva, but he didn't seem to care about that at all.

"It's completely mad," he laughed. "Absolutely mad." Another nut.

"I thought it would be much easier, actually."

"Mountain walking is never easy, but it's very good. Very pure. I think maybe you are crazy. But you made it here, so you will be fine. The first three days are the hardest. After, there is not so much pain."

Two women, both very pretty, joined us at the table. They were hiking for a few days and were on their way to the next town when they changed their minds and turned around. "It was so beautiful here, we came back," one said. They were Swiss, from somewhere on the other side of Lake Geneva. Bernard said something in French and they both aha-ed like some mystery had been solved.

One of the Swiss explained, "He said you come from New York and have never been in the mountains before."

I laughed. "That's mostly true."

"So," the other said. "Why do you come to the mountains?"

It should have been easy to explain. I'd asked myself the same question a million times, and in my head, I had rehearsed the answer *ad nauseam*, honed it to perfection. But what came out when I opened my mouth wasn't right at all—something about natural beauty and friendly people. *What am I saying?* I thought. What I wanted to say—what I should have said—was this: I had come to the mountains to walk. That part was simple; it was the main thing. I wanted to walk and walk and walk, obsessively, for days, to do nothing but walk and eat and sleep until I couldn't do it anymore. I wanted to know what it felt like to cover fifteen miles a day for weeks on end. I knew what five miles felt like, even ten—in New York I could easily cover ten miles in a day—but what about twenty or fifty or a hundred? And what about five hundred? Thinking about the distance made my head spin.

And I wanted to know why other people did it, too. Who are they? What is it about this walk that we find so appealing? I've always had an affinity for walkers, for nomads, for people who wander; people like Eric Newby and Peter Matthiessen and Robyn Davidson, and if I ever had the chance to meet them, I'd ask the same question: why?

But even if I'd said all that, it still wouldn't have been the right answer. Walking was only part of it. There were the mountains, too, and the journey itself. And then there was everything that came before—New York, Tokyo, Greece, the monastery—and before that—a decade of minor disappointments and missed opportunities, of aimless, unfocused travel. But you can't say any of that without sounding hopelessly sorry for yourself and obnoxiously self-absorbed. Who doesn't have regrets? Who wouldn't want a month in the mountains to "find yourself," as my brother jokingly put it? So it's not that, too, I told everyone in the room. I'm not here to soul-search. But it's something like that, maybe. Not a reset—a realignment.

And, I explained, I didn't want to suggest that I'm in any way special or that some great tragedy had sent me into the wild in search of Answers. Nothing like that. People do this all the time for fun; I knew that. But something drew me here, I said. I don't know what it is. But I have nothing to prove, not to myself or to anyone else. That was important, too. I'm not here to show anyone how strong I am, how much I can endure. Mostly, I said, again and again, I just want to walk.

They listened patiently as my answer dug itself deeper and deeper into incoherence and finally devolved into an apology for not being able to explain it in any way that made sense.

"You don't have to explain it so much" the Swiss said. "As long as you enjoy it. But it must be very boring here compared to New York."

"It's not boring. But it's quiet. Extraordinarily quiet," I said, "except for that helicopter."

"Terrible," she said. "It was a cyclist. She was unconscious. This happens sometimes, but it is terrible. People can be very dangerous. And there is no road, so a rescue must come by helicopter. It's the only way."

A herd of sheep walked by the refuge honking like old cars. An old man and a couple of dogs pushed them along from behind. The two girls spoke in French while Bernard studied his maps.

"Do you swim?" one asked.

"I can swim."

"I think we will go in the lake before dinner, if you would like to come. But it's very cold."

"I don't have anything to swim in," I said.

"Neither do we. It's no problem."

"Right, well, honestly, I'm not sure I can move my legs right now."

While we were sitting, my entire body had begun a process of locking itself up—perhaps some last ditch effort to keep me from walking myself to death. I pictured myself hobbling spastically into a freezing lake with two attractive Swiss girls, an image that was so ridiculous I laughed out loud. I would need my walking poles just to get over there. I put a little pressure on my right foot to test it. The pain was explosive.

"I'm sorry," I said. "I would love to join you, but its physically impossible for me to move right now. Bernard might even have to carry me to dinner."

She clicked her tongue and smiled. "Ah well. Another time, then."

Bernard and I watched them walk to the lake and duck out of view behind some large boulders. I tell this story not because it's a particularly good one, but because, inexplicably, it's true. There was a kind of magic to that evening that was completely unexpected, a freshness that came, I suspect, from being so far from anything or anyone I knew—from being, finally, in the mountains. It was enough to make me momentarily forget how much pain I was in.

Dinner could not have come fast enough. By half past six the only sound I could hear was a disgusting gurgling coming from my stomach. By seven o'clock I was so weak with hunger my body vibrated. Another man had shown up for the night and the five of us took our seats at the dinner table inside. A basket of fresh bread was brought out along with butter and vegetable soup. I ladled the soup in my bowl and sucked it down without tasting it. Then I sponged up every last drop with the bread and ate that, too. By the time the main course arrived, there was no stopping me. I tore into a giant slab of meat, set roughly on a plateful of pasta and carrots, as if I had never seen food before and might never see it again. When I'd succeeded in shoving the meat down my throat, I asked if I could have more.

"He likes it," Marie said.

"It's very good," I said. Though I probably could have eaten a piece of leather with salt and pepper on it and not noticed the difference.

"Do you recognize the meat?"

I slowed my chewing a bit to try and taste it.

"No, I don't," I said.

She pointed out the window to a field where a few dozen sheep were blithely gobbling up grass.

"It's the sheeps."

Bernard and the other man were totally unfazed by this revelation, but I was somewhat less accustomed to watching my food eat and eating it at the same time (much less watching it watch me).

"Mutton," Bernard said helpfully.

"Mutton," the girl said.

I looked at the sheep and chewed more slowly until I was staring into the wet, black eyes of one of the poor animals and moving my jaw in the same mindless oscillating motion. A small detachment had wandered to the wrong side of the lake and a dog was trying to bark them back. The dog moved in smaller and smaller circles until the sheep—fifteen or twenty, maybe—had nowhere to go but across a bridge that was missing its middle section. One after another the sheep leapt across the gap, each one barely catching the far end with its front legs before falling pathetically into the water. It didn't matter that not a single one made it; they just kept trying. Finally, one sheep managed to land with all four feet on the bridge, and we all cheered, but it looked so lost over there, so alone. The rest went into the water in quick succession, where they swam stupidly until they reached dry ground. Even the dog looked exasperated at such an astonishing display of ovine incompetence. We finished the meal quietly, either out of respect for the animals we were eating, or because we were too tired to speak.

I couldn't keep my eyes open. I had overworked and underfed my poor body all day, I hadn't had a proper night's sleep in days, and now I had gorged myself out of my mind on meat, pasta, soup, bread, butter, and water. My body was shutting itself down. Excusing myself from the table, I toddled back to the bedroom on horribly swollen feet and climbed into my corner. The room had no windows, only a small vent to let fresh air in. With the door shut, the darkness was thick and syrupy. I lay down on my back and, with my feet up, let a warm heavy feeling cover me like a blanket. I was so tired, more tired than I've ever been. I closed my eyes and pictured the sheep jumping idiotically, one after another, into the water. I may have even started counting them. But I didn't make it far before I fell into what had to be the deepest, most consuming sleep any human has ever experienced, a sleep so profound it was like hardly being alive.

6

I woke up the next morning as if I were coming out of a ten-year coma. Swimming through the sludge of my fatigue, I caught a noise that might have been a heart monitor or a car alarm or a tornado siren. It was muffled but distinct—a watch's wake-up call. I didn't recall setting the alarm on my watch. The noise stopped abruptly, but for a second or two I could still hear the high-pitched notes spiking like echoes in my ear. It was coming from the watch on the wrist of the man above me. After he switched the alarm off, I heard him roll over, as if he might snooze for five more minutes before he had to get up and go to work.

I opened my eyes to a room as black as the bottom of the ocean. I didn't move a muscle. More accurately, I didn't dare move a muscle because I was terrified of discovering that they no longer worked. I lay still and put my head together until I was sure I was awake. A faint brightness registered way off to my right; the outside light slipping in where a small vent didn't quite fit the wall. I was still on my back—I hadn't moved all night. I wiggled my toes and fingers. So far so good. But when I tried my legs, the pain was quick and scary, and I sucked a sharp breath to keep myself from crying out loud.

Propping myself up on my elbows, I tested the top half of my body. My shoulders screamed—my back was one large clenched muscle that wouldn't release. Having spent most of my life avoiding sports, hard physical labor, and anything else that might make me sore the next day, my experience with that level of bodily tenderness was very limited. The nearest I had ever felt to that sort of full-body hurt was the morning after I had spent a hundred-plus-degree July day moving myself and a roommate into a fifth-floor walk-up in Brooklyn. That night, I had collapsed in the middle of an IKEA bed frame that I was desperately trying to put together and woke up miserably sore and plastered to the hardwood floor the next afternoon. But here, on a hard mattress somewhere in Switzerland, I had to figure out how to get up and walk to another city.

Wincing, I pushed myself to the end of the bed and slowly lowered my feet to the ground. The floor should have been cold, but the feeling was like stepping down onto a bed of hot coals. In fact, nothing—not the soreness in my legs, not my bruised shoulders, and not the weird tightness in my wrists—could have prepared me for the breathtaking pain that blasted upward from the soles of my feet.

In his slightly insane diary of a walk from Munich to Paris, the filmmaker Werner Herzog writes that he "had no idea walking could hurt so much." I wouldn't have believed him until that morning and that moment. Walking sounds so benign, which is maybe why I prefer the word to hiking or trekking. We go for a walk. Something easy is a walk in the park, a cakewalk. But you really can't imagine the pain until you've felt it for yourself.

I had checked for blisters throughout the day and the night before, and remarkably, I didn't have any. The little research I had done on the Internet about hiking and incorrect hiking shoes had given me a pretty serious fear of blisters. (One reviewer of a pair of shoes I was looking at had the following to say: "Do not buy these unless you want to find alien-looking pus-filled boils on your feet and then you lance them and they become infected and ooze out through your socks. You will never walk again!!!")

But I had not developed a single bloody blister. That alone was a huge relief. It was the fiery pulses shooting out of my feet in regular intervals that concerned me. I wondered what the odds were that I had broken both my feet, if that was even possible. It occurred to me that I knew absolutely nothing about the composition of the foot and what injuries it might be susceptible to. I lifted one, and curled and flexed it. Bad, but not as bad. Then I tested it on the ground with some weight and saw stars. Supporting myself with the bed, I stood up, hobbled over to my bag, and swallowed four ibuprofens. It was a little past six and breakfast wasn't for another hour and a half. With my walking poles as crutches, I went outside into the light to have a look at what I imagined would be two horribly disfigured, swollen, purple pads.

They looked completely normal—no outward signs at all that would point to the pain. The air outside was cool and refreshing in the dawn light. I took a deep breath of it. After so many false starts and misfires, I realized, with no small amount of pride, that this was my first true morning in the mountains. And, despite the pain, I was happy to have it to myself, happy even to have been woken up by someone else's alarm. The sky bruised black, blue, and purple with a line of white building slowly in the east. The temperature was somewhere in the low fifties, and with each slight breeze I felt myself wake a little more. After a few minutes outside, for the first time in days—days that had felt like weeks—I wasn't the slightest bit tired or anxious or afraid or nervous. My pain was physical and it was manageable. The dread that had suffused the last week had subsided, and in its place was something as simple as it was surprising—pleasure.

Still, I was in bad shape. I had covered roughly thirteen miles, climbed five thousand feet, and descended two thousand the day before. My pack weighed roughly thirty pounds (I never got around to weighing it fully packed), which was probably too heavy. I felt beaten, hungry, dehydrated, and a little sick. But the biggest problem was that I had never actually done any of this before. I wondered if I was adaptable. Would there come a time when it would be easy? And how long would it take to get there?

Over breakfast—toast, jam, and coffee drunk from bowls—Bernard and I decided to walk together, which is to say he graciously invited me walk with him, since we were going to the same place, and I think he found my inexperience entertaining. I was grateful for the company, and thrilled to have found such an agreeable (and experienced) Frenchman to apprentice under for the day. I made it clear, though, that if he ever felt I was holding him back, he should just leave me behind. He laughed when I said that.

A quick good-bye to the Swiss girls, who were taking their time getting ready, and off we went past the lake and over the hill like characters in a French children's story. The path led gently through blooming, bright-green meadows under blue skies as the sun worked its way up over a wall of mountains in the distance—the Dents Blanches. Named, presumably, for their resemblance to the bottom row of one bad set of teeth, the Dents rise very suddenly to an altitude of nearly ten thousand feet on the French-Swiss border. Even from a distance, or perhaps especially from a distance, their height racked my nerves. They also looked impossibly far away, though I was pretty sure we would be passing them to get to Samoëns, a town back on the French side of the border.

By eight, the tenderized feeling in my feet dissipated enough for me to forget about it for a while. Bernard, who had noticed me limping early on, explained that this was normal and would go away after an hour or so of walking. "Walking," he said, "is the best remedy."

We crossed back into France at a border marked by an abandoned shed and a foot-high post with a quarter-inch line down the center—the exact line where the two nations meet. A white dog the size of a small horse approached us. He was old and moved slowly, but even an old dog that size was not an animal to piss off. There were sheep far down on the Swiss side, but the dog seemed far more interested in us. His brown eyes moved back and forth between Bernard and me. He didn't bark. I put out a hand, and he walked over and licked it clean. Then he turned toward France, put his forelegs on a higher rock and posed for pictures for a solid three minutes.

The heat that afternoon hit somewhere in the high nineties and became more and more draining as we dropped in altitude and entered the valley. By the time we reached Samoëns, an old ski town famous for its stonemasons (apparently even Napoleon used them for various projects), I was dangerously dehydrated, sunburnt (I had lost my sunscreen early in the day), and in a pretty bad mood (we'd spent at least an hour lost in some woods, walking in circles). I was having trouble thinking straight and walking for more than a minute or two at a time. In microscopic shuffles, I forced myself dramatically across concrete streets through the lively center of the city like a heat-stricken vagabond zombie in need of a bed and air-conditioning.

I told Bernard that, depending on how I felt in the morning, I may stay in Samoëns the next day to rest. He said that if I decided to continue walking I should meet him in the center of town at seven in the morning so we could leave together. In case I wouldn't see him again, I thanked him for the company and wished him luck. I found a cheap hotel on the far edge of town, ate dinner quickly, showered, and collapsed in the clean softness of a real bed. I dreamt that night of walking a thousand miles on flat ground.

I found Bernard right where he said he would be fifteen minutes after I was supposed to be there. He actually looked excited to see me, which was touching and encouraging. Especially since I almost didn't show. I had woken up late, around six-thirty, and stayed in bed for fifteen minutes debating. On the one hand, I could use the day to recover, give my feet and legs a rest, eat a lot, and sleep. On the other, I would miss a chance to walk again with Bernard, to hear about the life of a real mountain walker, and to do what I had come to do. Plus, I would have to pay for another night in the hotel. Thinking I had probably waited too long to meet him, but that I might still be able to catch up, I packed quickly and took off on my still-broken feet and stiff legs for the town center.

The whole village was asleep. The rhythmic sound of my walking poles, click-clicking like two blind man's canes against the cobblestones, was the only sound to be heard. Bernard, when

I saw him, was busy packing and repacking his bag, which, he said, was "entirely too 'evy."

"I'm sorry I'm late," I said.

"It's no problem. Actually we are waiting for another man. I met him last night at my hotel and he will walk today to Anterne with us. He went to find water, but he should be back soon."

"Perfect," I said. "How did you sleep?"

"Very good. I had a massage so I am feeling excellent today. My legs are like new." He tapped his legs with his poles and smiled.

"Where did you find a massage?"

"In the hotel. You did not have one?"

I did not, I explained. It hadn't even occurred to me, but I would have liked to, now that I thought about it. Bernard told me that it was not uncommon for hotels in the towns along the route to offer massages and that many walkers will get a massage as often as possible, sometimes every day. It was as much a part of the walk as the food, the wine, or the walking.

"You don't really rough it, do you?" I said, half to myself. "I like that."

"You should get a massage when you can. It is great for the legs. And you must drink mineral water. Perrier. For the minerals."

I was busy performing sad little stretches—the only kind of stretches I could do—when Michel turned up. Michel was around Bernard's age, short, a bit overweight, and already sweating. His clothes, which were slightly too large, and his backpack, which was slightly too small, gave him the sweet look of a schoolboy ill-equipped for a weekend camping trip. When he spoke to Bernard, his fleshy features and droopy eyelids became exaggerated, like a mime without the white makeup. Bernard introduced us. Michel apologized for not speaking English, and I apologized for not speaking French. "We're in France, after all," I said. Bernard translated and Michel shrugged in agreement.

"He will be good practice for you," Bernard said.

Under the loose leadership of Bernard, we made our way back into the wild. Riverside walking gave way to steep switchbacks through thick forest where steel ladders had been screwed into two-story-tall boulders. The climbing was intense, and Michel and I, usually trailing Bernard by about fifty feet, had to take frequent breaks to rest and catch our breath. Each time I stopped, Michel looked very relieved to have an excuse to break, too. Low, gray clouds kept us cool, but the moisture in the air made the ground oil-slick and more dangerous than I was in the mood for on day three. A few exposed downhill stretches on wet leaves turned my stomach upside down. I took these very, very slowly. So slowly, in fact, that Bernard and Michel both laughed at me.

"It's his first time in the mountains," Bernard said at one point to an audience of patient day-hikers who were stuck behind me.

We stopped at a café that was perched on a high rock next to a waterfall. The waterfall, which was bisected by a paved road, is something of a tourist attraction in the area, and the morning buzzed with people who had driven up to take pictures, eat lunch, and drive home. How strange to emerge from the woods onto a road full of people and cars. You can't hear the sound until you are almost at the tree line. The woods are like an insulated world, protected and quiet. The noise of people, the smell of cars—they come through just barely, as if filtered or absorbed by the trees and the ground, by the earth itself. Even the roar of the waterfall is dull until you are just under it.

An hour and a half later, we were climbing the lower of two major cols that day. The walk could be measured in cols, the low shoulders between two high peaks. These are the passes that allow a walker to cross through the mountain at all. The route—any mountain route, really—flows up and over cols like trade winds over the surface of the sea. Bernard kept his pace until he was far enough ahead that I was sure Michel and I wouldn't catch up for the rest of the day. A light rain spat down on us intermittently, and we paused every fifteen minutes for water, or to put our rain jackets on or take them off. At the top of the col, we could see a cluster of low buildings in a large flat valley.

"*Le refuge*," I said. But Michel disagreed. The refuge was on the other side of the next col. Those buildings were another refuge.

"*Déjeuner*. Perhaps." He shrugged.

We staggered in from the rain and found Bernard spread out on a hard wooden bench inside the hut, his hat tilted rakishly over his eyes. He'd been there for about forty-five minutes and had already eaten. Much like the hut in Switzerland, the interior of this one was closer to a spruced-up woodshed than even the most basic hostel. But it was warm and dry, and I was cold and wet. The head-to-toe ache that had plagued me the day before had weakened enough that I could ignore it as long as I was walking (probably thanks to the ibuprofen I was eating like candy); however, as soon as I stopped to sit down, it came roaring back: shoulders, back, legs, feet, all on various degrees of fire. Lowering myself to the table, I worried about not being able to stand up again.

Refuge Alfred Wills has been operational since the early eighties, but the story behind the name goes back a bit further. It was here, a hundred and sixty-five years before I arrived, that a British climber and author—Alfred Wills—happened upon a remarkably pristine valley. Understandably impressed by its beauty, he described it in a guide to the area as "at once so grand and so full of softer beauty . . . even amongst the Alps a very miracle of beauty." Wills, in an effort to make the place more popular with British climbers (who were quickly spreading across the mountains of Europe in what would become known as the golden age of alpinism), got the idea of building a chalet there. He called it the Eagle's Nest (also the name of one of Wills's books about his Alpine exploits). Despite a very busy decade of climbing, which included an ascent of the Wetterhorn, Wills eventually built the chalet. It stood, uninhabited for years, until it was looted and damaged during World War II. I did this research on Wills much later, though at the time the name sounded vaguely familiar—some scarp of alpine history I'd read and tucked away and was now trying to dig up, to put to use. But I couldn't focus right now. Dozens of flies were landing and lifting off my body and some crumbs of food on the table in a hypnotizing show of insect aeronautics. I was also very hungry.

Michel ordered soup, which he said was the best thing to eat for lunch—juice was best for breakfast and meat was best for dinner. I got *la croûte*, which I was both warned about ("very heavy for walking") and encouraged to try ("very good"). Explaining even the most basic national dishes can be difficult, and my two friends struggled to tell me exactly what *la croûte* was, even though it's fairly simple: a crust of country bread soaked and cooked in cream and eggs and covered with melted cheese. It came to me in a piping hot casserole dish, and I ate it quickly as soon as it was cool enough. That it would be a digestive nightmare later on was almost a guarantee, but that didn't stop me from scraping every last bit of cheese from the dish. Lunch that day was one of the most satisfying and memorable meals of my life. Months later, I can still taste the salty, gooey cheese, the warm cream, and the sour bread. And the effect on my body was extraordinary. I felt brand new, like I could walk another four hours if I wanted to—a good thing considering I had almost exactly four hours of walking ahead of me.

After we finished eating, Bernard left me and Michel to get a head start to the next refuge, which, he said, was "just over the next col." Michel fell asleep in the exact same position as the one Bernard was in when we had found him. I spent forty-five minutes prodding my sore muscles to see where the pain felt worst.

The sky was miraculously clear when we left; the only trace of the afternoon's rain were the slick rocks under our feet. I spotted Bernard high above, near the top of the pass. An hour, I figured, to climb to where he was, about fifteen hundred feet above. That felt doable, but only because I didn't have a good sense yet of how much time and energy was required to cover that much ground. The path climbed gently at first and then more aggressively the higher we went until it was like climbing an endless flight of stairs, a thousand feet below and a thousand more to go. My legs lit up with every step. Michel struggled, too. We must have looked ridiculous, straining so hard to climb what was, in contrast to the mountains around us, such a small hill.

Like a mirage, the top of the pass kept moving farther away. Whenever I thought I had the end in sight, another higher path would reveal itself. The letdown each time this happened was more devastating than the last. Near what I hoped was the real and final top, I sat down (then lay down) to wait for Michel. He caught up to me half an hour later and collapsed on the soft grass like a dead horse. When I stood to stretch my legs, I walked up the path without my pack for a minute or two to try to get an idea of how much longer this would take. What I found was breathtaking: across the sky—the distance was impossible to determine—and above the hills was a line of snow-covered peaks bigger, taller, and more massive than anything I had ever seen. Where the clouds broke, light glinted off the steel-black rock. The mountains rescaled the world around me and I stared at them, gobsmacked and dumbfounded, like I had discovered them. And in some sense, I had. At one point, the clouds parted enough for me to see what I was looking at; in a flash, I recognized it from pictures, like a celebrity I'd only ever seen in magazines: Mont Blanc, *le toit de l'Europe*—the roof of Europe.

I walked down to get Michel, who had fallen asleep flat on his back in some high grass. Afraid he might sleep until tomorrow, I rustled some items in my backpack until he opened his eyes and sat up.

"*Regardez*," I said, pointing up the hill. We walked up, and when the mountains were in sight I said, "Mont Blanc." Michel looked at me like I'd just pointed to a tree and said, "tree." He had, of course, seen the mountain before, but turning toward the peak, even he couldn't help but smile at it.

The trail descended steeply down the far side of the col in sharp zigzags that I could only see once I was on them. The ground was wet from weather, and my feet threatened to slide out from under me. Michel, who was much faster than I was on downhills, waited every few minutes for me to catch up. We would exchange a quick "*ça va*" and carry on down the mountain. By the time the ground finally flattened, my legs trembled like jackhammers. My knees, which had made it through the first couple of days unscathed, felt seriously wrong, like the bones were scraping against each other. But I was close, for the third time in as many days, to my destination. And I was alive.

The refuge, set deep in a stunning valley ringed by high peaks, was even more remote than the first night's. We dragged ourselves inside at around seven in the evening, far too late. Bernard was drinking tea outside when we arrived and, again, he looked genuinely happy to see us. "Mont Blanc," he said, pointing to the towering pyramid of ice and rock above us.

"It's really incredible," I said. "I've never see mountains like this."

"Tomorrow we will be even closer. It will be a very hard day, but we will be close to the mountains. It is spectacular where we are going." His eyes twinkled in the cobalt evening light, like the glaciers above us.

During dinner—sausage and polenta—we made plans to wake up the next day at five a.m. The reason, Bernard explained, was that much of the climbing would come early in the day and it would be best to get it done before the afternoon got too hot. Five in the morning sounded ridiculously early to me, and I knew from my limited experience that it would be pitch black. But who was I to question anyone? Plus, Michel seemed fine with it, so I held my tongue. I will admit, though, that the thought of us leaving in darkness, headlamps lighting the way, was wonderfully romantic. And there was no way I wouldn't fall asleep as soon as I hit the bed anyway.

The three of us watched through a window as the light faded on Mont Blanc. When it became dark enough, we spotted two or three dim lights high on the mountain—huts for summiting climbers. They reminded me of lighthouses, but they couldn't help but look out of place—temporary, like the mountain could shake them off when it realized they were there. Just thinking of a night in one of those places made me feel cold. Those were thoughts for another time, though. For now, I was warm and tired and full and, surprisingly, looking forward to the next day.

7

The Brévent rises to a little more than eight thousand feet above sea level, high enough to give Chamonix, far down in the valley below, the clean plastic sheen of a toy village, but not quite high enough to take anything off Mont Blanc. A cable car connects the Brévent to Chamonix and ferries tourists from all over the world up to the top for the view. The trail, on the other hand, spills up onto the Brévent by way of a kind of back door, so that all of a sudden you are hiking with color-coordinated teams of silver-haired Japanese women, French families with small children, and, perhaps oddest of all, the unmistakable sound of American English.

Our predawn wake-up hadn't really panned out. It was too dark and cold to leave. So we sat over coffee and juice in the dining room for an hour until it seemed light enough to go outside.

Before we could climb to the Brévent, the main event of the day, we first had to descend deep into a valley. And for every step down the mountain, there is, invariably, a step up later on. On a small patch of land at the bottom, we passed a young German couple that had camped for the night next to a powerful river. They had the wonderfully relaxed look of two people for whom camping next to a river under the tallest mountain in Europe was the most normal thing in the world.

"It's not a good idea to sleep there," Bernard said after we'd passed.

"Why?" I asked. "Because the river could flood?"

"No. Because it's too loud. I could never sleep with that noise."

The climb, like all climbing, was miserable—long, painful, and relentlessly steep. The whole way up, Michel wore the unpleasant, sweaty look of a religious pilgrim on his way to salvation. I stopped as often as I could to eat through a stash of sugar jellies I had picked up in town a couple of days before. They were all that was keeping me alive. If I went too long without one, I felt like a vibrating mass of soft, rubbery limbs. Bernard had already gone ahead of us almost as soon as the climbing started and Michel fell behind me soon after, leaving me completely alone for the first time in what felt like days.

Two-thirds of the way up, I rounded a corner and found six chamois lying on a small piece of land that stood like an island away from the mountain proper. The area is famous for its wildlife, but other than a thousand marmots, which are the ground squirrels of the Alps, I hadn't seen anything. The chamois, a mid-sized antelope-like animal found in the mountains of Southern Europe, is well adapted to life at high altitude—so I read—but I still couldn't figure out how they had gotten out there. Or how they would get back.

Slightly farther on, the Mont Blanc massif, having been obscured for most of the day by the Brévent itself, came into full view for the first time since we'd left the refuge. A crowd of hikers, including Bernard, were sitting on rocks looking across the valley at the mountains. People swapped cameras and took pictures of one another squinting into the sun with the peaks in the background. I have a picture of myself here, taken by a stranger. I'm smiling and standing straight. I look healthy, which is not at all how I felt. But pictures have a way of telling a better version of the truth, one that's closer to an ideal than the actual memory could ever be. In the back of the photo, you can see paragliders frozen in midflight. When I look at the picture, I find the paragliders and remember, with pleasure, watching them float in lazy circles around me. Bernard and I ate lunch there while we waited for Michel. When he caught up, we pushed on.

On one especially memorable section of the climb, I had to use both hands to hold onto the rock face. Any small slip could have sent someone (me) down to the bottom of the mountain to die a rocky, scree-filled death. Needless to say, it scared the shit out of me. With the laser focus of a brain surgeon, I moved my hands to only the most solid-looking rocks. When I was sure I had a hold that wouldn't slip out, I moved my feet over. I did this many times over until I felt I had the hang of it. Then, a rock dislodged under my right foot. I hugged the mountain, my heart rate jolting up to the speed of a hummingbird's. I covered the entire section, maybe a hundred feet, methodically, as if my life depended on it (which it did). Any unnecessary movements, anything that could throw off the little balance I had—especially with the weight of my pack pulling me off the wall—were kept to an absolute minimum. Bernard stayed close to make sure I could actually get through it. When I did (finally), he beamed with fatherly pride.

"*Ça va?*" he asked.

"*Ça va,*" I lied.

A group of people, mostly old people, had collected and were waiting for me to finish before they could start. Once I was done, they skipped across like it was nothing.

But the hard part was over, at least for now, and I could get back to worrying about other things. Like the sun, which, without any shade around, was baking us stupid. I poured water on my head every few feet, hoping a breeze might blow through and cool me down. It never did. I wasn't carrying enough water to waste anyway, so I settled on tiny sips every other minute. The ground had turned into flat, gray gravel that sent little clouds of bone-dry dust up with each step. Traffic thickened near the top, and at one point I was marching in step with a group of Asian tourists on their way from the cable car to a viewing platform that offered completely unobstructed views of the whole Mont Blanc massif. It reminded me of getting lost in Manhattan and ending up in a street parade in Chinatown that you can't find your way out of.

At the very top, I took in the view like everyone else. The Mont Blanc massif features a number of iconic peaks—the Drus (where James Salter set the best part of the best mountain climbing novel ever written), the Grandes Jorasses, the Aiguille du Midi. They stretch out in every direction, impossibly high. It was here—at what now marks the triple-border between France, Italy, and Switzerland—that the Alps had reared up and grown higher than anything else in Europe; here that the colossal fragments of the earth's crust had collided and, with nowhere else to go, pushed skyward. If it's in a mountain's nature to rise—to climb up through the wind, water, and time—then the massif is the Alps' crowning achievement. For someone who, until the day before, had never truly seen mountains, it was a powerful vision. Had I not been so tired and hungry and sunbaked, I might have, like the tiny old Chinese man next to me, been moved to tears. Instead, I took a few pictures with my phone and sat down in a sliver of shade under the awning of a small building, an information booth that had some displays devoted to the local flora and fauna. When the shade disappeared a few minutes later, I went inside and cut up slices of salami next to a taxidermic marmot.

The cable car, while not strictly in the spirit of adventure, was too tempting to not consider. A quick meeting between the three of us confirmed what each of us suspected individually: no one wanted to walk down the mountain, not in the heat, and not after the day's climb. Even the book seemed to warn against it, noting that the path "zigzags down a rough and rocky slope," and then adding nonchalantly that "a length of rail protects against overshooting a sudden left turn . . ."

Ten minutes and ten euros later, we were in Chamonix drinking beer while Michel weighed the pros and cons of hiring a taxi to Les Houches. Michel was tired, he said. And his legs hurt. He'd worked hard enough already, so there was no reason to push it. It would be a boring walk anyway—two hours of flat streetwalking between cities with no view. To my own astonishment, I told Bernard that if he felt like walking, I'd be happy to walk with him. I probably felt guilty about the cable car. Not as guilty as I did about the bus a few days before, but guilty enough to walk a couple more hours in the afternoon heat.

It was slightly off-route, but the walk was not unpleasant. The trail cut west through Chamonix, out of the suburbs, and mostly followed the easy winding path of the Arve, which receives water from the Mer de Glace glacier on Mont Blanc itself and flows all the way back to Geneva, which right then felt a world away. The glaciers of Mont Blanc, like bright shining tongues, glistened brilliantly on our left.

We made incredible time, covering what should have taken two hours in about an hour and fifteen minutes. Every so often, Bernard would say something to himself and laugh. His good spirit was infectious, and even I began to feel pretty happy about being out there walking. The anxiety of climbing, the height, the heat, the pain, the guilt of cheating—all of it fell away until the world, or my world at least, became spectacularly small: the path, Bernard, the next step. Everything else was some distant component of a different life, and none of it mattered.

It was my last night with Bernard and Michel—they were continuing on the next day and I had decided, in a weak moment to myself back on the Brévent, to rest a day in Les Houches. When I stopped moving, my feet still felt broken. Or if not broken exactly, defective. And downhill walking was painfully slow because of the stabbing in my knees. I had been walking for four days without a rest (in retrospect, four relatively hard days), and the thought of a day spent in bed, reading, taking notes, and wandering around some small, calendar-perfect town was too good. I also wanted to eat as much as I could. Once we got close to Les Houches, I told Bernard I wouldn't be going with them the next day. He said it was a good idea. I must rest, he said, and take my time; it's not a race. After we made plans to meet that evening for dinner at a proper restaurant—with menus—I left him at his hotel to find a place to sleep for the night.

The town, a strip of small hotels and shops stretched along a main street, had all the requisite quaintness of a ski village at the foot of Mont Blanc. The boulangerie was a few blocks from the fromagerie, which was not far from the church, which was a stone's throw away from a mountain museum. The jagged peaks of the Mont Blanc massif loomed overheard, but the sight of it was softened by the angle, the view somehow less menacing from the town than it was from the Brévent. After a lot of awkward inquiries about rates and availability, I found a hotel that was far cheaper than the rest for reasons I never found out, though I think it was explained to me in French—something about renovations. If it was a noise problem, I was sure I would sleep too deeply to notice.

At dinner a couple hours later, Bernard raised a glass of wine.

"It is French wine," he said. "France has the best wine in the world."

I agreed.

"To the mountains." We touched glasses and drank. Bernard was in an even better mood now that he'd had his massage, and even though Michel looked like he was falling apart, he swore he felt great (he'd had a massage, too). But I was uneasy, stuck inside my head, looking forward to my day off tomorrow but anxious about leaving such good companions behind. Or rather, letting them leave me behind. My intention had been to do this alone, and the idea didn't bother me, but so far I'd only been alone for a day. The truth is that it was good to have company, people to talk to. In between bites of *coq au vin*, I asked what brought them to walk through the Alps—why would they leave their families, I wondered, just to toil up and down mountains on their own. What did they get out of it? These were regular guys with jobs, wives, and kids, but they approached this less like an adventure than a vacation. I asked what their families said when they heard the plans.

"They were very happy," Bernard said.

"They didn't think it was crazy?"

"In France, it's common to go to the mountains to walk. It's a very old tradition. These paths have been used since Napoleon, since the Romans. They don't want to walk, my family, but they think it's quite good for me. Some coworkers perhaps think it's crazy. But they don't know mountains. They are from the city and know only the city. They don't know the routes, the Alps, the Pyrenees. But for some, if you have seen the mountains, you must walk them. This is me."

Michel, in broken English, agreed with everything Bernard said. And I couldn't argue, although I'm certain members of my family already thought I was crazy. But Bernard was right, I had seen the mountains, and now I had to walk them.

Back at their hotel, we said farewell and they wished me good luck. Bernard gave me his phone number and told me to keep in touch and to let him know if I needed anything. He told me to look him up if I ever visited Paris. I said I would, touched by his kindness over the last few days. I wished him luck as well. With no rest days, his walk would be far more difficult than mine. But Bernard was built like an ox; he would be fine. Michel shook my hand warmly and said it was nice to walk with me. I replied that it would be weird to walk alone, but Bernard assured me I would meet more people on the way.

"We come alone," Bernard said. "But we know we will be with other walkers. It's part of the tradition. You will see."

I stayed in bed until noon the next day, then left to eat lunch and see the town. At a cheese shop, which smelled like a cave that hadn't been cleaned in centuries, I explained that I was walking to Nice and needed a cheese that would keep well without refrigeration.

"Anything in the Gruyère family will be perfect," the man behind the counter said.

"Who's in the Gruyère family?"

"I have many. I will give you the best," he said cutting a chunk from a wheel and wrapping it up in brown paper for me. "You can keep this for a week in your bag, no problem."

"A week?"

"It will keep for longer, but you will eat it before that. I promise."

I made a trip back to Chamonix by bus to buy some supplies—a charger for my phone (mine had mysteriously disappeared), sunscreen, some energy bars—and was already feeling better when, at a café, the sun came out from behind the clouds and saturated the valley, the mountains, and the city in a thick golden light. I was sitting outside on a narrow street without much foot traffic. I lifted my face to the heavens and closed my eyes. I must have fallen asleep like that, because the next thing I remember is a waitress asking me if I was okay. The street had cleared out and the shadows were long on the shiny cobblestones.

Back in my hotel room, I drifted in out and of sleep until the light outside was gone. It was pleasant to be alone in my own room, half asleep, thinking about how the only thing I needed to do the next day, and the day after, and many days after that, was to wake up, walk, and sleep. Life hadn't been this simple in ages. I almost felt guilty about it.

8

The path out of Les Houches climbs a low ski hill before it leaves the world behind and dips back into the wild. The first part of the climb stuck to a semipaved gravel road that was being serviced noisily by a large fleet of trucks. They kicked thick clouds of dust up in my face each time one passed. At an old railway stop near the top of the hill, a middle-aged man with leather-brown skin approached as I was refilling my water bottle. He gestured and spoke too quickly for me to understand. I told him I didn't really speak French.

"Ah, sorry. I thought you were French," he said, switching to perfect English. "England?"

"No, I'm American."

"American! Very good. Look, we are sorry about the dust. You were walking in the dust because of our trucks."

"Oh, it's no problem," I said. "Dust, rain, heat. It's all the same. What kind of work are you doing?"

"Trees," he said, as if that explained it. "You are walking? Tour du Mont Blanc?"

"I'm walking, but not the Tour du Mont Blanc. I just left Les Houches this morning."

"And where will you go?"

"I'm trying to go to Nice. I started near Lac Léman."

"Are you sure you are not French?!" he laughed. "It's a beautiful walk. I've done many of the routes around here."

"Is it hard?"

"Yes. But you look strong. You should not think about the difficulty; this is not important. The mountains are important. The nature. The people. The difficulty is only temporary."

He was smiled kindly at me, and I at him. He wished me good luck and stuck a hand out to shake. I wondered if he would disappear into one of his dust clouds if I touched him. But after I shook his hand, he just turned around and walked away.

The weather, which was essentially the only variable that mattered each day, was perfect. More perfect weather could not have existed. It was sunny and cool in the shade, windless, and cloudless. The sky was a pristine blue, and the light on the mountains turned the view in every direction into a gorgeously rendered landscape painting. I walked along, lost in the rambling thoughts that accompany walkers—thoughts that, if they were ever spoken aloud, would not make a shred of sense. The ground stayed mostly flat after the initial climb, and for this I was extremely thankful. My feet were bad—though not as bad as they had been, which meant that they might actually be getting better or at least adjusting—but my lower back (a new pain) and shoulders were hurting. And my knees screamed loud and clear on any downhill stretch no matter how soft the grade.

I stopped for a coffee in a village of eight or nine houses. A group of children on horses passed me and waved. I thought of Bernard and Michel, who had most likely stopped in the exact spot the day before. Then I remembered Bernard telling me that if the weather was good (which it was) he was likely going to take a different, more difficult route, because the views were better. Would I ever get to the point where I would take the more difficult route for the better views? Had I ever in my life made a decision like that?

I made it to the Col de Voza at fifty-four hundred feet after about two hours of walking. This was, according to the book (which I was now checking with an obsessive regularity), roughly on schedule. The col was the highest point of the day, which was good insofar as I didn't have to climb anymore, but bad since going down is the more painful of the two directions. Since I had started walking, I had heard some version of "when you are climbing you wish for a descent and when you are descending you wish for a climb" countless times. It may be the most frustrating and true statement there is about walking through mountains. I panted and cursed on the way up, but as soon as the land tilted toward the sea, I missed the smooth muscular movement of climbing. Descending is closer to a kind of controlled and prolonged fall; there is no grace in going down—only clumsy steps on canted ground.

The hamlet of Bionnassay is one of hundreds of tiny storybook mountain villages in the Alps that look too good to be true. Rustic stone buildings sit in a high valley surrounded by ice-covered peaks. A few farmers mill about, slowly pushing animals this way and that. They are not in any rush. It's the kind of place that makes disappearing from your old life and starting a new one seem like a reasonable plan. How hard would it be to find a home here? Land some work? Live cheaply? Live a simple life?

There are hazards, of course. On a July night in 1892, the Tête Rousse Glacier, which sits on the Mont Blanc massif above the valley, collapsed and released an estimated 200,000 cubic meters of floodwater on the villages below. Bionnassay was completely destroyed, wiped clean off the map. Accounts report the loss of around two hundred lives in an instant.

I continued downhill, mostly on schedule. Despite an uphill slog at the end, I made it to Les Contamines ahead of time and with energy to spare. I picked up a large, bready lunch in a boulangerie and ate in the shade near the visitors' center. At one o'clock, the sun was climbing and the heat was becoming difficult to ignore. I put my head under a fountain to cool down. It felt too early to stop for the night, so I checked the book for the hundredth time that day and found a hut about an hour and a half away. The walk didn't look too steep on the chart (it never does). I thought, do I risk it? Risk what, exactly? What the hell, I thought, this is an adventure, after all.

The route turned out to be very steep, very boring, very hot, and very painful. It stuck mostly to crumbling rocks that slid back with each step. The sun hung directly overhead. It took closer to three hours to get to the hut, rather than the hoped-for one and a half. The trail ran through a busy tourist spot over a gorge that was so crowded with elderly people—all of whom were in better shape than I—that I didn't even try to squeeze in to see what I imagined was just water gushing out of the rock. I heard it, though, which felt good enough.

I arrived at three-thirty—early compared to the last few days—tired, burned, and sore, but proud of myself for pushing my limits a little. After some fruit juice in the shade, I felt fantastic. Dinner wouldn't be ready for another three hours, so I settled into a lawn chair and put my feet up to read.

In the past few days, I felt like I had gained a bit of a rhythm out in the mountains. I had walked enough and seen enough that I could reasonably predict how the next few weeks would go, to a certain degree at least. It was a relief to know, basically, what was in store. It lightened my mental load considerably and, more important, made it possible to read more than a few lines of a book before nodding off or falling into a dark pit of anxiety. I decided to shelve *War and Peace* for the time being. The book had too much to pay attention to. Instead, I decided, I would stick to short books, stories about mountains, or walking, stories I could relate to.

Which is how I came to start skimming Nan Shepherd's *The Living Mountain.* I had thrown the book on my e-reader without knowing much about it—only that it was short and that the author had spent much her life walking the Cairngorms in Scotland. It turned out to be a magnificent little book—I read the whole of it in one sitting—full of poetry and, on virtually every other page, sentences so lovely I smiled reading them. Sentences like this one: "Light in Scotland has a quality I have not met elsewhere. It is luminous without being fierce, penetrating to immense distances with an effortless intensity." And this: "Water so clear cannot be imagined, but must be seen. One must go back, and back again, to look at it, for in the interval memory refuses to recreate its brightness." I could go on like this for a while, but suffice it to say that, that afternoon, with the Alps towering over me, the book struck a chord.

Sitting outside the refuge, I read page after page with a goofily tickled expression on my face. Then I came to Shepherd's description of a climber she knew. "What he values," she writes, "is a task that, demanding of him all he has and is, absorbs and so releases him entirely." I liked it so much I copied it in my notebook. I couldn't have put it better; it was precisely how I felt—absorbed and released, daily. Not just physically exhausted by the end of the day, but emptied. And then, almost miraculously, renewed enough the next morning to do it all again. My task each day was so simple: walk to the next checkpoint, get myself over or through whatever ground lay in my way. The path was already plotted—all I had to do was follow it.

I turned my book off and turned my eyes up toward the mountains. I wanted to hold the idea in my head for a little while, to let it soak through me. A man walked up to me and asked if I knew when the rest of my group would arrive.

"My group? I'm alone."

"You are not the group of Americans?"

"I'm afraid not."

"But you are American, no?"

"Yes, but I'm here alone. Not with a group."

"I see. So you do not know when they will arrive?"

"I don't even know who they are."

"They are from New York."

"I'm sorry, but that doesn't help."

"No problem, no problem," he said.

There was, in fact, a group of Americans, and being American myself I was made a member for the night. We were seated together for dinner, given our own room, and treated as one five-headed, non-French-speaking American tourist. They were unfailingly nice people, all around twenty years old and full of the stories American college students pick up when they travel in Europe for the first time. They were doing the Tour du Mont Blanc, a ten- to fourteen-day circuit around the Mont Blanc massif. I had not heard of it until the day before when the book warned that the next few days would overlap with the route and become very crowded. But the last thing I expected was to have dinner with people from

Florida, Illinois, and Ohio (no one was from New York). They complained of always being put together and apart from the rest of the guests. When I asked if they spoke French, one girl said she'd been learning for the last few days, and after a few glasses of wine her recitation of a few phrases cracked us up like children. Even the French across the room laughed.

I woke up slightly hung over the next morning. Outside my window, a luminous sunrise filled the sky with an otherworldly blood-orange and purple glow. The light looked thick enough to swim through. I walked out of the hut to take a few pictures, but they came out either too dark or too light. Fussing with my camera, I thought of something else Shepherd wrote, about the mind not always believing what it's taken away. I made a mental note to look up the quote later, then realized I probably wouldn't remember the mental note. This felt like a perfectly Shepherdian circuit to start my morning with, and I took it as a sign—because I needed signs—that the day would go well.

The man who ran the refuge came outside to join me. I asked if he had a weather report for the day. He said it would be good, possibly rainy in the afternoon. I supposed that was all right, though it would have been better without the rain. I would move quickly, I thought. Beat the rain. But I knew that even if I moved as fast as I could (which isn't that fast), the rain would come when it came. I could do no more to beat the rain than I could to turn back time or flatten the earth beneath me. The man went inside and came back with two cups of coffee. He sipped his slowly, taking deep breaths before putting the mug to his mouth and letting out a satisfied *ahhh* once he swallowed it. He squinted into the distance as if he were starring in his own coffee commercial, and the morning light cut deep creases into his face.

"This refuge is beautiful," I said. "You're lucky to wake up to this every day."

"It has been in the family for five generations! Over one hundred years!"

I couldn't think of anything to say except that I hoped it stayed in the family for another hundred years. But it sounded too dramatic, so I didn't say it.

Later, I found a website that confirmed the man's story in delightfully broken English: "In 1870, his [Joseph Alexandre Mattel's, the owner of the properties on the site] son Joseph converted the family farm into a hotel. Then it was the turn of Gustave Mattel (son of Joseph) to continue the running of it, then Abel Mattel (son of Gustave), then in 1976 Lucienne Mattel (daughter of Abel) and latterly in 2001 Patricia Mattel (niece of Lucienne)." In case you weren't sure it had remained in the family throughout this string of handovers, it concludes, rather definitively, "The Nant Borrant chalet has always belonged to the Mattel family." Also included in this origin story is an almost too-French-to-be-true sentence from the original council's decision on the establishment of the inn: "Considering that the people obliged to cross this mountain are very exposed because there is no seller of wine or groceries, the aforesaid council has unanimously decided that it is very urgent to establish, on the Nant Borrant site, a site very favorable and agreeable for foreigners, an inn-keeper who will sell wine. . . ."

After breakfast, I said good-bye to my new American friends—they were heading in the opposite direction—and for the seventh (or sixth? I couldn't do the math anymore) time, I walked out of a hut due south, never to return, though not ungrateful to have slept in an inn that would sell wine to people like myself, who are obliged to cross this mountain.

9

I stopped to rest near a concrete bunker that looked like it had seen some action in World War II but had been left to crumble ever since. Between measured sips of water, I skimmed the book. Climbing, descending, climbing, eating, sleeping, descending—a loop that went on as long as I wanted it to. Jesus, I thought, every day from here to the ocean looked exactly the same. The terrain alternated between woods, meadows, and bare rock, but for the most part, one day's walk looked a hell of a lot like all the others. I skipped around the book, searching pages from days and weeks ahead, trying to find something to look forward to.

I turned back to the route I was to take today and found a paragraph I had somehow missed: "The walk along the Crête des Gittes is inadvisable in very strong wind, or if snow and ice covers the path." The Crête des Gittes, I read, is a high, narrow ridge on the far side of the already high pass I had to cross that day. The path lies on the needle-fine point of a rocky triangle that drops dangerously on both sides. A photograph in the book of two smiling hikers preparing to cross made my stomach turn. I looked into the distance to see if I could see it, but all I saw were mountains. Then I remembered that rain had been forecast for the afternoon. Did a warning against crossing in strong wind also apply to crossing in rain? I sat for a minute and thought about turning back to wait for better weather. But the weather was already perfect. The people at the refuge would laugh me off the mountain. Keep walking, I thought. Keep walking. Always, no matter what, keep walking.

So I walked, slowly, toward the Col du Bonhomme—the col before the Crête—which was still hours away. A Frenchman who was walking with his wife and two young daughters caught up to me later in the morning. He was alone. He and his family had stayed at the same refuge last night, and I had managed to speak with the him for a few minutes before the guests were separated by nationality. He was in his forties and, like most everyone else I met, fit enough to run circles around me. Not surprisingly, so were his wife and daughters. They were the picture of a French mountain climbing family: blond hair falling on the heavy packs they shouldered without complaint as they bounded up and down the mountains. They were on the Tour du Mont Blanc, he told me. It was his fourth time around, his wife's second or third, but his kids' first. When he was younger, he had completed the circuit faster, in about six days, by running long stretches of it. But now they would take about two weeks, depending. (Depending on what, I'm not sure, since they all looked more than capable of crossing the entire country in two weeks.)

While he waited for his family to catch up, I asked if he had ever crossed the Crête des Gittes.

"No," he said, looking at the picture in my book, "but it looks amazing."

"It looks scary," I said. "What if I slip?"

"Don't slip."

"But it's supposed to rain this afternoon and my book warns against crossing in bad weather."

He craned his head up at the sky, which was so clear it looked incapable of ever producing clouds at all.

"I don't think it will rain. Just walk quickly. And don't slip."

Buoyed by our talk, I left him to wait for his family. The path had climbed high enough that I'd crossed the tree line a while back. It felt nice to be out of the woods for the day. As long as it didn't get too hot, the high mountains were preferable if for no other reason than the incredible views. (When it did get too hot, of course, I couldn't have cared less about the views.)

With the sun still rising, the mountains to the south organized themselves in fading silver ridges as far as I could see. To my right, a massive peak—probably the Aiguilles de la Pennaz—shot theatrically into the sky. I could see ice high up on the mountains to the left. Before me, the trail dipped and rose softly over green hills, an unbroken white line three feet wide and pocked with millions of holes left by walking sticks. I had read that the path I was walking was on one of the old salt routes that stretched from the ports in the south to all parts of France. For centuries, caravans had moved across the same lines and seen the same peaks and valleys, the same plots of land, and the same chalets and rivers. History had literally been walked into the ground, and I was adding another layer to the story—a micron-thin, totally inconsequential layer, but a layer nonetheless.

I reached the Col du Bonhomme around nine thirty a.m. I was making excellent time, and there was a chance I could be across the Crête des Gittes before the afternoon rain started. A sad little monument displayed the altitude (2,329 meters, or almost eight thousand feet) and gave the times needed to reach various points on the trail. But as far as I could tell, all of the places listed were behind me. Suddenly, I felt very lost. I checked the book again. I was in the right place, an hour from the Croix du Bonhomme three hundred feet above me. Once there, I would have no choice but to step onto the ridge and put my life in the hands of the mountain. (Actually, that's not entirely true: there is an alternate path that follows the Tour du Mont Blanc to Les Chapieux where you can take a road and reconnect to the route I was on. Although this was mentioned very clearly in my guide book, I didn't notice it until weeks later. It's hard to say if it would have made any difference.)

I was sitting with my back against the monument, lost in doomsday weather predictions—a smear of white clouds had appeared in the sky, way off to the east—when the French family came running up the mountain behind me. The father shook my hand, helped me to my feet, and congratulated me on making it to the col. I hadn't thought of it as an achievement worthy of congratulations, but why not? We'd made it. It was hard work—more than three thousand feet in only a couple of hours. And it was gorgeous. I'd congratulated people on far less impressive feats, and anyway, I felt good. My legs were still stiff and rusty in the morning, but after an hour of climbing, they practically pulsed with strength. Standing on the col with only three hundred feet of climbing ahead, I was sure I could run the rest of the way. Of course, I didn't try.

We walked up a steep slab of rock together, the kids jumping like goats, to the Croix du Bonhomme. We crossed a small stream, and, in formation, they each whipped out their water bottles to refill them with what seemed to me dangerously suspect water. I sipped at mine slowly, careful not to empty it. After a short, slippery climb to the top, we all shook hands and they peeled down the mountain to the left while I looked ahead in terror. I held the photo of the Crête up and compared it to the real thing. The photographer must have worked hard at making it look less scary, because from where I was standing, it seemed impossible to cross without falling. Plus, clouds were actually gathering now in purple-gray popcorn kernels directly above. The sky darkened. My stomach sank. A trio of middle-aged men passed by and climbed to the start of the ridge. I hurried to catch up, thinking it would be better to tag along with perfect strangers, particularly French strangers, than to go it alone.

Nearly level with the top of the ridge, the trail, just barely scraped out of the side of the mountain, looked incredibly long, like it would never end. A slip, if you couldn't catch yourself in time, might truly mean tumbling clear down to the bottom. I tried not to think about that. I tried, instead, to think about how good it would feel at the other end. I tried to think about how unlikely it was that I would actually fall. After all, I had never heard of anyone falling from the Crête des Gittes. (Never mind that I had never even heard of the Crête des Gittes until earlier that day.) I tried to think about the ocean, the way the water would feel on my scorched skin. I did not look down, or up, or off to the sides. I kept my eyes on the path ahead of me, on the back of the feet of the men in front of me.

The men moved quickly, easily. It was nothing to them. They could have been on a day hike for all I knew and would be crossing back the other way later that afternoon, rain or shine, or maybe the next day on their way home. They were free to enjoy this in a way that I was not. At least not yet. I hadn't earned it, hadn't spent enough time in the mountains. So, for the time being, I was stuck suffering through it. The path rose and fell; we climbed and descended fifteen, twenty feet each time. It stuck to the east side of the mountain, then switched to the west. I lost track of time, but I must have been on it for half an hour before I could see what I hoped was the end. When I got there ten minutes later, it was not the end but another in a series of blind climbs to another stretch of the ridge. Finally, the line stopped abruptly and fell hundreds of feet in short, sharp zigzags down the mountain. Here, I thought. Here is where I fall and die. An old man asked if he could go ahead of me and said to take my time, be careful, "go slow, go slow." Slow it was. Painfully, dreadfully slow, as I placed each foot on the ground, tested the rocks below for slippage, and held my breath when I shifted my weight. Every few steps I slipped anyway, a fraction of an inch, which isn't much, but it's enough. I looked back. Again, a line of hikers had formed behind me. I stepped aside to let them pass, which they did with big, bouncy steps. I could see people at the bottom, so small from this high up. Halfway down, my knees were in serious pain. There must be a technique for descending steep trails, I thought, but I didn't know it. My arms were starting to cramp, too, from the force I put on my walking sticks when I stabbed them murderously into the ground. I was a wreck. When I finally took the last step off the ridge onto a big, flat patch of soft grass, I collapsed in a pile of dead limbs and sweat-drenched clothes. The three men who started with me applauded and raised their water bottles in my direction. One walked over to me and handed me a candy bar.

I ate my lunch like a starved soldier. I calmed my jittery nerves with sandwiches and peanut butter and chocolate. I looked up at the Crête and could hardly believe I had crossed it. The book downplays the walk, calling it a "fine stretch" and boiling the death-defying descent down to five plain words: "zigzag down to a col." But it felt much bigger than that, more challenging and therefore more rewarding, something that had taken all my concentration and all my physical coordination and that left me shaking and empty at the other end. In the euphoric relief of not being up on the path anymore, I lost track of the clouds, which were now blotting the sky completely. Lying on my back in the soft grass, I closed my eyes and felt cool drops of rain land on my skin.

When the sky finally opened up, the storm, which had been steadily gathering strength all afternoon, turned out to be a monster. Fortunately, I had made it to the hut by then, having walked through a few light mists for the last three hours of the day. Now, looking out the greasy window, I saw nothing but water, sheets of it. Claps of thunder rattled the small hut and flashes of lightning lit the room like a broken strobe light. After each bright burst, I saw neon images of mountains everywhere I looked.

Aside from being relatively dry (there were a few leaks), the situation inside the hut was dim. Though the room was full of people, no one spoke, neither to me nor to one another. It seemed like I'd wandered off the mountain into a house of mourning. A family, presumably the owner's, sat sullenly around a table looking at one another or at nothing at all. I heard some French, but nothing above a whisper. A baby cried from what sounded like somewhere outside, but no one seemed to care. I looked at a map on the wall, then thumbed through a few old magazines on a bookshelf. But I couldn't ignore the odd sense that people were looking at me when my back was turned. Maybe I'd done something wrong. True, they were a little miffed that I had shown up without a reservation, but there was still plenty of time to make preparations for dinner. And as far as I could tell, I was the only guest.

The hut was one long, low rectangle, divided haphazardly into three sections: kitchen, dining room, dormitory. Every piece of furniture looked as though it had been made of spare scraps of firewood at the last possible minute, then repaired a dozen times since. At one end was the toilet and shower, which you had to go outside to get to, and at the other a small covered deck, on which an old man was smoking a cigarette that he had to block with one hand to keep from getting soaked with rain. It was the only dry spot on his entire body.

I never figured out what was going on in the hut but I was anxious to remove myself from whatever I had walked into. I unrolled my sleeping bag on my bed and lay down. Even in the early evening, the sleeping area was dark enough that I could barely make out the slats running across the bottom of the bunk above me. Then I started to worry that if I fell asleep, I'd miss dinner, so I propped my head up on a wooden beam and laced my fingers below it. I looked to my right and saw two bright eyes staring at me from a bed across the room. They belonged to a gentleman who had apparently been watching me the whole time.

Seeing me see him, he spoke. "*Bonjour.*"

"*Bonjour.*"

"English, Dutch, German?"

"American. How could you tell I wasn't French?"

"Your accent. I knew *immediately* you were not French."

"I only said one word."

"That is all it takes." He sat up in his bed. "Do you speak French?"

"I'm afraid not, but I'm learning."

"Wonderful," he said, extending his hand. "*Je m'appelle Daniel.*"

"*Je m'appelle Jon,*" I said. "Nice to meet you."

Daniel was in his sixties and was dressed like he was ready for a round of golf and drinks at the club: khaki trousers, a white polo, and a thick cable-knit sweater thrown over his neck and tied loosely in front. He had been lying down in this getup at least since I arrived. After our high-school French introductions, the conversation dead-ended and I went back to staring at the bed above me. I was certain, though, that Daniel's bright eyes were on me the whole time. When I snuck a quick look, he was, invariably, looking at me and smirking.

Creepy as that was, it was nothing compared to the hulking, hooded figure who burst through the door an hour later, drenched and backlit by bolts of lightning. He wore shorts, which was odd, to say the least, and a thick, possibly homemade woolen sweatshirt with a tall, pointy hood. His boots seemed to be as old as I, and his pack was even older and held together by frayed lengths of rope and a lot of tape. A patchy beard and long hair rounded out the picture. He was given a bed—the third bunk—where he promptly stripped down to his underwear, draped his wet clothes over various pieces of furniture, and went to sleep. Daniel, finding my eyes in the dark, raised his eyebrows questioningly. The baby started crying again, and a young waif-like woman slipped through a crack in one of the walls to what could not have been bigger than a small closet. She managed to quiet the baby, just in time for the dinner bell, which set the baby off again.

The three of us ate in silence. Daniel looked at me every so often and smiled while the other man pored over charts and maps and took tiny notes in a tiny rain-blotched, water-logged notebook like someone lost at sea. After the second glass of wine, Daniel started talking. He had driven here, he said. There was a car park down the road. Did I not see it on the way in? He had hoped to do some light walking but the rain had come out of nowhere. He would wait and see what the weather looked like in the morning, though he would probably just come back next week, he said. Or he might stay the next day and see. He was a retired chemist. He asked what I was doing out here in the mountains, so far from America, and when I told him about the walk he said he had never heard of the route. He was sure it didn't exist. When I showed him the book, he admitted it was possible but that no French person would attempt such a walk. I told him that almost everyone I had met so far along the route was French. Here, the man with the charts and maps chimed in and said it was quite popular with French people. We left it at that and went back to looking at the window, hoping for the storm to pass, which it showed no sign of doing. Not to be brought down by a silly argument, Daniel went back to smiling at me a couple minutes later.

10

I slept fitfully, waking every half hour to check if the rain had stopped. Morning dawned dark, gray, and wet through the little window across from my bed. I checked my watch. Five-thirty. I could probably leave as late as eleven and still make it the full distance without having to walk in the dark. Or, worse comes to worst, I could stay another night and hope for better weather tomorrow. But I wasn't sure I could take another day there. Walking in the rain would almost certainly be preferable.

"Where are you going?" It was the man with the charts.

"Valezan," I said.

"I go the same way," he said gruffly.

"What about the rain?"

"It is a problem."

"Yes. It seems to be."

"Here," he said, spreading out one of his military-grade survey maps. "This could be bad in the rain."

I couldn't make much sense of the lines, which swooped and swirled this way and that, but I trusted him. I would have trusted anyone with maps like that.

"*Dangereux*," he whispered.

"So you will wait here today?"

"No."

"So you will walk?" I pointed at the map, my finger on the *point dangereux*.

"No."

"Is there a third option?"

He dug for the word and when he couldn't find it, stuck his thumb out sideways.

"Hitchhike?"

"*Oui.* 'Itch 'ike."

It was hard to picture anyone stopping their car for him, deranged as he looked in his shorts and pointy hood. There was a road, he explained, back the way we came. It was fairly busy and led, indirectly but eventually, to Valezan. He showed me a thin blue-black line on the map that curled from close to where we were to close to where we needed to go. At this point, Daniel joined us.

"Today," he announced looking at his phone, "it will rain." He showed us the forecast. Rain all day—thunder, lightning, the whole thing. "But perhaps it will be clear around noon." He showed us another forecast from another weather service, and indeed, it showed perfect yellow sunshine from midday on. "Rain? Sun? We do not know," he concluded helpfully.

The man and I turned back to the map—huddled over it like prisoners plotting a breakout.

"So you will try to get a ride?"

"Perhaps I will cross *la montagne*."

"But you just said it was *dangereux*."

"*Oui.*"

By the time we stepped out of the hut, the rain had slowed to a drizzle but horrifying clouds were amassing in every direction. They were also coming out of the ground in giant gray-white drifts.

The man pointed south and started walking. I waited, then followed him. An adventure, I thought. And what was adventure without danger? But fifteen minutes later when the rain started coming down in earnest, I had second thoughts. Namely: why was I following a probably crazy man I did not know over a mountain in categorically dangerous conditions?

"*Monseiur*," I shouted. He was thirty feet ahead of me and hadn't looked back once. "Are you sure about this?"

"*La montagne*," he said, extending his walking pole toward the peaks.

"Yes, I know, but are you sure it's a good idea? Shouldn't we take the road? What if there is lightning while we're on the mountain? That must be stupid, right?"

"But it's too late. We are already in the mountain."

"Well we're only an hour from the road, probably less."

"No, no. I will go on. But please, take the road if you do not want to cross the mountain."

"You are going to Valezan, yes?" I said, having made up my mind to turn back to the road. "I will look for you there."

"*Bonne chance*," he shouted through the deafening din of the rain slapping against the rocks.

I turned around. A herd of beautiful caramel-brown cows had gathered on the path and were working the soft ground into a pool of mud and shit. These were the Beaufort cows I had read about somewhere, famed for the rich milk they produce, milk that is then used to make the Beaufort cheese the region is famous for. (We had eaten platefuls of it the night before, and to be fair to my otherwise prickly hosts, the cheese was delicious—every bit as buttery and rich as they say.) The cows watched through wet eyes as I headed back toward the hut, stopped, changed my mind, walked to catch up with the man, stopped again, turned back toward the hut, and finally disappeared into a cloud of mist. Were they judging me? I wondered. Probably.

I had no trouble finding the road, but the rain kept stopping just as I was about to give up and stick my thumb out. I was determined to walk as long as the weather wasn't absolutely dreadful, which it mostly was. I had a good rain jacket with a hood and a rain cover for my pack, but my pants were soaked and water was saturating my socks. I walked for two or three hours on the pavement while the storm failed to make up its mind about whether to drizzle or pour. Sometimes it managed both at the same time.

After many miserably wet miles, I stuck my thumb out. But even that was wishful thinking since no more than five cars had passed me the whole morning. Then, within three minutes, a large white van pulled over and a man who looked a few years younger than I rolled down the passenger window. He and the driver stared at me.

"Valezan?" I tried it in my best French accent.

The driver spoke, in English: "We are going to Bourg St. Maurice. From there you can take a bus to Landry and perhaps another bus from there to Valezan. This weather is shit for walking."

"Yes. It is shit," I agreed. "Wherever you are going sounds good."

I stuffed myself in the front seat and apologized for my wet clothes, but they didn't seem to care.

"All the shit is wet in this shit weather," the driver—Robert—exclaimed. He was pissed, he said, because he, his cousin (also Robert), and some friends had planned a weekend in the mountains. The weather was supposed to be good, and then it wasn't. It was shit. All they wanted to do was hike, drink, and look at the stars. But with the clouds, they couldn't see anything, so they had spent the night in the van and were now driving home. Robert the driver was twenty-eight and a woodworker. Robert the cousin was twenty-five and training to become a doctor in Lyon. Impressed by my plans to walk to Nice, they both said I had made the right decision to hitchhike. I told them about the man with the charts. The cousin clicked his tongue and said, "Foolish."

"It's shit today," the driver repeated.

"Do you like *génépy*?" the cousin asked me.

"I don't know what it is."

"It's for drinking," the driver explained.

"I don't think I've had it."

They lapsed into quiet French between themselves.

"Would you like to try?"

"You have some here?"

"No, at our home. Robert makes his own, so we have a lot. It is best when it is house made."

"It always is," I said. Everywhere in the world, but especially in the country, people believe the local drink is best in its moonshine variety. They swear by it and it's impossible to argue. Also, I knew better than to turn down such an invitation. Once, I nearly brought a grown Albanian man to tears, out of his good eye at least, when I declined a sip of his *rakia* for fear of contagious disease and because the two-liter bottle he was trying to put to my lips smelled like manure (no doubt the secret ingredient in his family's recipe).

"If you think I'll have time to make it to Valezan," I said. "Sure."

"You will like it. It is made only here in the mountains. Very local. It is, like, the national drink. So you must try it. And Robert makes it very good," the cousin said.

"Perfect."

As we drove down twisting mountain roads at forty miles an hour, my thoughts turned sympathetically to the man with the charts. No doubt he was battling wind and rain, alone up on the mountain in nothing but a wool sweatshirt and shorts like some lost teenager making his long, lonesome way home. And here I was, almost dry, in a warm car with two fun-loving cousins named Robert. With any luck, I would walk into the *auberge* in Valezan and see the man hunched over his maps, pencil and notebook in hand.

Robert the driver placed the jar ritualistically in the middle of the table. It held a pale yellow-gold liquid and a few mangled sprigs of something that had been stuffed roughly inside, presumably for flavor, but possibly to add to the presentation. It looked a little like urine, but cloudier. It did not look like something I wanted to drink. One of the cousins unscrewed the lid and held it to my nose. I sniffed gently, but not gently enough. My nose burned and my eyes started watering. I jerked my head backwards. They both laughed because recoil is the international signal that moonshine has been made right.

"What is it?"

"Alcohol."

"Right, but what's in it."

"Alcohol, mostly. Pure alcohol. Then I add to it sugar and this plant. I don't know what it is called in English. I pull the plant myself. It grows only high in the mountains, and you are not supposed to pull it. But I pull it."

Three glasses were poured and we toasted to the mountains. I sipped cautiously. Surprisingly, it wasn't all that bad, which was a relief. The last thing I wanted to do was spend the day drunk and the night sick, and then wake up blind. It was slightly sweet, but full of flavor, something like absinthe. (I found out of a few days later that it is related to absinthe through their shared use of wormwood.) While we drank, Robert the woodworker showed off pieces he had made: pens, picture frames, glasses cases, dishes. He had also done all the cabinets and much of the furniture in the house. Left to his own devices, he might have rebuilt everything out of fine woods.

"Are you hungry?" he asked.

I was, and so lunch was prepared. We kept drinking through the meal until the jar was empty and another was brought out. I remember mentioning how unpleasant the hangover would be, especially since I still had to walk several miles that day, but neither of them seemed concerned. The bus, they said, leaves a bit later. I would make it in plenty of time. Another jar appeared.

I don't know how long I was there, but at some point Robert the cousin made some coffee and said he would drive me to the bus station in town. I thanked both of them for the food and complimented their génépy, which really was good. We remarked on the good fortune of our meeting, though I'm not sure what they got out of it, except maybe the chance to share their booze. They wished me luck on my journey to Nice. "Think of us when you drink génépy," the driver said, suddenly making the whole thing oddly moving. I said I would, and I did.

Anyone who has traveled will have stories of chance meetings with uncommonly warm locals whose only wish, it seems, is to please bumbling tourists. In my experience, these occurrences are relatively rare. But when it happens—when you are plucked off the road in the rain and cooked for, and when you drink and talk with people you never dreamed of meeting—it's a true gift. The selfless kindness of strangers when you least expect it is one of the treasures of travel that never fails to impress me. Sadly, I did not get any contact information from either Robert, so it's unlikely I will ever hear from them again. Which is fine, in a way—as if it were all a dream.

I waited at the bus station, slightly wobbly, for over an hour and a half for the next ride to Landry. The rain had mostly stopped, but to the east ash-black clouds were still tossing lightning back and forth. The cousins had packed some food for me in a red-and-white-checked cloth tied with twine. It was heavy. I untied the twine and unfolded the cloth to find a chunk of bread, a giant wedge of Beaufort cheese, and a glass jar of homemade *pâté*. The *pâté* looked inedible, but the bread and cheese were manna from heaven. Suddenly, I was a starving. I took greedy bites of the bread, then the cheese, until both were half gone. Then I realized they would have to last until dinner, possibly later if I didn't make it to the auberge in Valezan in time. I wrapped them back in the cloth and tucked the package in my bag. I felt like Laurie Lee, on his away across Spain on foot with nothing but his violin and a rucksack, except I didn't have a violin, and I was waiting for a bus.

Landry, it turned out, was a very short distance from Bourg St. Maurice. In the time it took to wait for the bus, I could have walked there and back. Fifteen minutes after boarding, the bus deposited me at an abandoned train station on the north side of the village. I consulted my maps. Landry was actually on the route, but I wasn't supposed to be there until the next day, which meant I would have to move in the wrong direction back to Valezan and then double back tomorrow to Landry. In principle, this was extremely frustrating, but I had no choice. I had an appointment in Landry the next day and there was no place to sleep there that night.

On my map, Valezan looked really close, just on the north side of the river and uphill past another small town. I still had plenty of light left in the day, and the weather was holding. I crossed the tracks and cut across a flat pasture. The sun sliced through the clouds and spotted the ground with bright green circles. I walked along a stream for half a mile or so and turned north at a bridge. After a muggy morning walking on pavement, and a lot of génépy, it felt good to be out in the fresh air. It felt good to be walking, too, until I remembered I was moving backwards. Perhaps that was why the climb to Valezan, once it started, felt so punishing. The path was terribly steep and made mostly of muddy wooded trails. I lost track of the red-and-white markings in one of the small villages it passed through and spent more than an hour climbing a path on the wrong side of a deep gorge. I went back down, found the right way, and started up again, but my blood boiled from having wasted so much energy.

The final stretch into Valezan climbed out of woods through someone's backyard. Rain was coming down again, and my clothes, which had finally dried in the brief periods of after-noon sun, became damp and stuck to my skin. I donned my rain jacket, which didn't breathe well, and eventually it got too hot and uncomfortable, and I took it off, despite the rain. Now I was wet and tired, but that seemed better than being wet and tired and hot.

Maybe it was just the clouds and the rain, but Valezan was depressing—a heap of big farmhouses with corrugated steel roofs and a bunch of chickens walking around. I didn't see any people, either, until I startled a woman when I rounded a corner. I asked if she knew where the auberge was, and she pointed further uphill.

Had I been moving south—that is, in the right direction— the auberge would have been wonderfully convenient. As it was, it was at the very top of the town, which meant climbing today and descending tomorrow.

All these bitter feelings disappeared, though, when the staff of the auberge led me upstairs, unlocked my room, and revealed it to me as if it were the presidential suite at the Waldorf. The bed (there was only one) was a cloud of soft, dry sheets. The thought of slipping into them was almost too much. A door opened up to a terrace that offered unbroken views of the mountains to the south (at least I'd be sleeping in the right direction, I thought). Better yet, the bathroom featured not just a shower but a tub. And best of all, it didn't cost any more than a filthy bunk in some barn out in the mountains.

The manager, a kind woman with almost no English, patiently told me in French to come down for dinner around seven fifteen and, either satisfied that I understood or sure I never would, excused herself. I stood in the center of the room in my rank, damp clothes with my pack still on my shoulders. I stayed like that for a while and listened to the breeze coming in, the sound of the floor creaking. I closed my eyes and slept for a minute standing up, like a tired horse.

After a shower and a long soak in the bath, I went down for dinner. A table had been set up just for me. I'm not sure there is anything lonelier than a table set for one. For a moment, I missed the communal dining rooms and crowded tables of the rougher places in mountains, awkward as they may be. I don't think I had eaten alone since the second or third day, and it felt strangely quiet to be sitting there. I was lost in these melancholy thoughts when I spotted a very familiar set of threadbare boots clomping down the stairs. We both lit up like long-lost friends.

"You made it!"

"*Oui*, and you too." We shook hands and I gladly gave him the empty seat at my table. Wine was ordered.

"Well," I said. "How was it?"

"*Très dur*," he said, leaning across the table. A votive candle lit his face but his eyes were dark. "*Très excitant!*"

"Scary?"

"*Oui*. I fell many times. The storm was all around. I could not see in front of myself. And you?"

I mumbled through mouthfuls of food about hitchhiking to Bourg St. Maurice, the cousins, the génépy, the bus. But as good as my day was, I couldn't help but think I should have followed him into the storm. I'd turned my back on the mountains, on adventure. I'd acted cowardly; I'd done the very thing I was trying not to do. How much cleaner would the sheets seem after a day like his? How much better would the bath feel? How much more miraculous would every sunny day seem after walking up into a thunderstorm and back down out of it?

The man—I never learned his name—said he was glad I made it to Valezan, and we both toasted to better weather. Eventually the conversation wound its way back to his walk that day. He described the details for me in broken English and children's French, but I had no trouble at all picturing it: the leaky shack he holed up in soon after I turned back when the rain was really coming down; the muddy pastures that sucked the boots off his feet; the crumbly limestone he slipped and scrambled his way up; the bone-rattling volume of the thunder exploding only a few feet overhead; the blinding flashes of lightning; the brief moments when the rain stopped and it felt like the clouds were gathering their strength for another round; the path, visible only a few feet at a time and sometimes disappearing altogether; the solitude of standing atop the Col du Bresson at eight thousand feet in a storm; the truck-sized boulders he passed that were sprinkled like salt down the mountain a million years ago; the speed with which he moved when he knew he was close to the end; the hunger he felt since he hadn't stopped for lunch; the relief when he saw the town—it was indescribable. "*Il n'y a pas de mots*," he said. There are no words. He showed me the network of scrapes and bruises he had acquired on his arms and legs.

I asked where he was headed tomorrow. He laughed.

"Home."

Part Two
Wayfinding

11

For all my talk of going it alone, the truth is that I asked nearly everyone I know to come with me. I started with my brother, pitched it to him as an epic adventure, a complete escape from the drudgery of his regular life as a Park Slope–living graphic designer with a nice apartment and a good job. It almost worked, too. But then that good job wouldn't have been there for him when he got back.

Most of my good friends enjoy regular employment, and even if they don't they had some other reason they couldn't go— kids, weddings, vacations already planned. All fine reasons. I don't blame them. I'm sure I sounded slightly crazed. No one really thought I'd go through with it anyway; I wasn't even sure I'd go through with it. Everyone assured me that, if the circum- stances were different, if the timing were better, if work were less busy, if money weren't an issue—it sounded like a lot of fun. I even floated the idea of asking my parents to go, but I was afraid the walk might actually kill them. It was only once everyone had turned me down that I seriously considered going alone. Alone could be good, I thought. Alone could be quiet. Then again, alone could be insane.

Maybe that's why it didn't occur to me to ask Colin, even though I've known him since high school. We grew up down the street from each other in our little south Kansas City bubble and were roommates the whole time I lived in New York. Who knows? Maybe sometimes you can't see what's right in front of you; you take certain things for granted; you make assumptions about people. When I finally did think to mention the trip to him, I sent a quick email from a café in Zagreb with a basic schedule and a few pictures of the French Alps. He replied that he was planning a long vacation in Europe around then—something I have never know him to do—and might be able to join for a week or ten days. I read the reply a few times to make sure I got it right. I could barely believe it. In fact, until he stepped off the bus in Landry, I still didn't believe it.

Organizing our meeting in France was a complicated, old-school affair that involved a primary plan and several backup plans in case any of the dates and rendezvous points shifted. Since I wasn't sure exactly how long it would take to get to Landry—a blip of a town that happens to be on the walking route and on a major railway line—I gave him my best guess. If I wasn't there when he arrived, he would just have to wait.

To get to Landry, he would fly from New York to Paris and then to Lyon, take a train and then, at some point, a bus to Landry. I figured I wouldn't have a lot of access to the Internet in the days leading up to our meeting, so last-minute adjustments were out of the question. Once the operation was set in motion, we had no choice but to hope for the best. I liked the pre-Internet pliability of our plans. Nothing was set in stone or locked down to the minute with flight numbers and air-port codes and pickup times. In all likelihood, we would both arrive around the same day—and if we didn't, no big deal. It reminded me, in a vague way, of the part in Nicholas Bouvier's *The Way of the World* where the author and his friend, having set off from Belgrade on an epic road trip across the Middle East and into Central Asia, find themselves hopelessly snowed in in some small town in Azerbaijan for an entire winter. "The life of a nomad is surprising," Bouvier writes. "You cover nine hundred miles in two weeks: the whole of Anatolia in a cloud of dust. . . . Then you yawn, stretch out, fall asleep. In the night, the snow falls, covering roofs, smothering shouts, cutting off roads . . . and thus you spend six months in Tabriz, Azerbai-jan." Here is one of the key differences between touring and traveling: the former requires all sorts of plans to be locked in place, while the latter acknowledges—even embraces—how lit-tle regard the world has for our hard schedules, our rigid time-tables, our desire for predictability.

Before I left for Geneva, I called Colin and told him that I would email if I could, but that if he didn't hear from me to count on meeting in Landry around the tenth of August. I did manage to get a strong Wi-Fi signal a few days in and shot off an alarming message about how difficult the walking was, how I might have underestimated the whole thing, and how I'd been wrong about most of the gear I said he would need. "Get a good backpack with strong hip straps," I wrote, along with a list of many other items I was worried I had overlooked. After I hit *send,* I realized I had left something off: "Oh, and walking sticks are a MUST." Sent. Then one more: "Don't let these emails scare you. It's great out here. We'll have a lot of fun. See you soon." I never heard back.

From Valezan, I retraced my steps to Landry. The sky was crystalline. Only the softness of the ground hinted at yesterday's rain. Rather than leave everything to chance (which is my default plan) and end up sleeping under the shelter at the bus station, Colin had booked us ahead of time at a small bed and breakfast. I had no trouble finding it at the top of the hill on the south side of the town, but when I rang the buzzer, no one answered. It was early in the day, so it was possible that everyone was still asleep. It's France, after all. Fortunately, my walking for the day was done, which was a huge relief. I walked to the back of the building and peeked in a few windows. No one was around. I left my bag under some stairs, grabbed my ebook, and headed back toward the river, which flows east-west back at the north end of the town.

The place was deserted. Shops were shuttered, restaurants (both of them) looked like they hadn't been open since the late eighties, and a weed-filled lot with a sign advertising sporting activities stood empty save for a dilapidated trailer that was almost completely rusted through. The only sign of life was an old woman vigorously sweeping the ground in front of her door. She had been sweeping, I guessed, for no less than thirty years. She eyed me with unbridled suspicion.

I settled into a nice spot by the river where, even in the sun, the air was ten degrees cooler. I turned on my ebook and the battery promptly died. With nothing else to read and no means of charging it until I got inside the hotel, I napped. Thirty minutes later, I walked to the bus station to check the timetable. The train, if Colin was even on it, was supposed to arrive at three thirty that afternoon, in six hours. Back at the hotel, no one was up yet. A sign on the door instructed guests who arrived before noon to call a number. Of course, I didn't have a phone that worked without an Internet signal, and I couldn't find anywhere in town that had even heard of Wi-Fi, let alone provided it. The only thing I could do was wait, something I hadn't had to do since I started walking.

It was painful, sitting around with nothing to do. Normally I'm really good at waiting; I'm one of the most patient people you will ever meet. But in Landry, waiting was torture. Swapping my depleted e-reader for the guide book, I went back to the river to read up on what the mountains had in store for the next twenty-odd days. But my eyes glazed over, and I ended up scanning snippets of one section over and over again: "Think ahead when accommodation options become sparse, such as around Plan de la Lai . . . and over the Col du Bresson to Valezan. . . . A bit of advance planning could save a lot of wasted time and frustration." I had not thought ahead. Nor had I read this part of the book. I flipped ahead to the next few days, and indeed, options for eating and sleeping cropped up fewer and farther between. I had a tent with me, but it was only big enough for one person. And I doubted Colin would bring his own. I sunk into a bit of a panic, imagining the two us of curled up under the overhanging roof of a refuge, frozen and wet. I cursed myself for not bringing a phone and for not doing my research. Then again, maybe Colin would find the whole not-knowing-where-we-would-sleep aspect exciting. Plus, I had never heard of anyone being turned away from a refuge. At worst, they make you sleep on the floor. I remembered Bernard telling me that refuges used to be free and, in the past, were rarely staffed. The idea of turning someone out was impossible, he said. It would be terrible. No one—no French—would do this.

Feeling a little better, I went to find some food. One of the restaurants had opened and was actually serving breakfast. I ordered the largest omelette they had and, feeling much better, went off to check the hotel again. Landry is small, but it's built on a hill with the river at the bottom and the hotel at the top. This meant that each time I went to check on the hotel, I had to climb up the hill, which triggered the pain in my legs. With no one at the hotel yet, I climbed farther up the hill to a church, but the door was locked. The clock tower on the church rang at noon when I was right under it.

I spent the next three hours repeating the morning's loop: river, hotel, river, hotel. Every once in a while, I walked to the train station to make sure everything was on time. By three, I was cracking up with boredom. It had also gotten very warm, and I had to scrounge around down by the river like a marmot looking for shade.

No train came at three thirty, though the screen displaying the timetable apparently thought it did. It confidently blinked "arrived" and moved on to the next train. At four, a bus unloaded a few college students who made a beeline for the display screen and looked disappointed when they read what it said. I asked one of them if they were coming from Lyon. Geneva, he said— Lyon was the next bus, in five minutes. Thirty minutes later a bus pulled in, but no one got off and the bus drove off without an explanation. A few minutes past four, a small coach slipped into the station, deposited a single passenger, and sped off with a cloud of dirt behind it.

Colin and I grinned stupidly at each other across the parking lot. He was dressed somewhere between a boy scout and a rookie park ranger—khaki shorts, khaki shirt, pristine hiking boots, and sparkling new backpack. In contrast, I looked like I had spent the last week sleeping in a ditch by the river, my clothes stiff with dirt and dried sweat, and my skin burned in bright red patches. I had a wide-brimmed sunhat on and wasn't wearing my glasses (I had stuffed them down to the bottom of my pack days before), so I had to squint to see him. Crossing the dirt lot to each other, we shook hands and laughed. The last time I had seen him was on a bittersweet blustery January night in New York, the night before I had left for Tokyo. Neither of us, nor anyone else in the world, would have had us meeting again six months later in southeastern France to hike through the Alps.

Colin is a big guy, well over six feet tall, with the solid build and youthful features of an overly friendly high school football player. In most rooms, he stands slightly hunched, like he's used to finding himself in small spaces. I couldn't wait to bring him to mountains, to show them off like they were mine.

"Welcome to France," I said.

"Thanks. It's good to be here."

"Did you get my emails?"

"Yeah, but they didn't make any sense. And I'd already bought all my stuff."

"Well, don't worry. We'll sort everything out."

"Is there a lot to sort out?"

"I'm not sure. I've been locked out of the hotel all morning, so I don't have any Internet."

"What have you been doing?"

"Sitting. Waiting."

"For how long?"

"Hours. I got here really early this morning."

"Eesh."

"How do you feel?"

"Great. You?"

"Great. Except everything hurts."

"That rough?"

"You'll see."

"You keep warning me. Should I be worried?"

"No, no. It's not that bad. The first few days are pretty bad, but after day five or six it gets much easier."

"I think I'm only here for seven days."

"That's not much time, is it?"

When we got up the hill, the hotel was still unstaffed. I tried knocking again, but no one came. Colin tried. Nothing. Then he noticed that the door was unlocked (it may have been unlocked the whole time), so we pushed it open and let ourselves in. Tiptoeing up a flight of stairs and into a kitchen, we startled a woman with headphones corked into her ears.

"Sorry," I said. "Is anyone working here?"

"I am." She spoke with an accent, Australian maybe, and looked at me with the biggest, blankest eyes I have ever seen.

"We've been knocking for a while."

"I guess I didn't hear you," she explained.

"No, I guess not."

"I'm not supposed to have anyone coming today. Did you call ahead?"

"No. I don't have a phone. We made the reservation online."

"Through the website?"

"I don't remember. My friend did it."

"The website doesn't work sometimes."

"I think it was through a booking site."

"You should have booked through the website. You get a better rate."

"Do you have a room?"

"I don't know. Let me have a look and see."

She walked away and I looked over at Colin, who was held rapt by a giant plastic relief map of the area.

"They have those all over," I said. "They make the mountains look much smaller than they really are. Nothing seems as hard on those. Probably a good thing."

She came back and said, "I have a room for two, but it's quite pink."

"I'm sure it's fine."

She was not lying about the room. Not only was it quite pink, it was also adorably decorated with lots of small pillows and puffy hearts and lacy curtains. I placed my muddy bag and walking sticks in a corner as delicately as I could, careful not to soil the whole room.

"Also," I said. "I have a favor to ask. I'm afraid the refuge we are supposed to get to tomorrow will be full before we get there."

"You want to call ahead?"

"It's just that my French is pretty bad, and over the phone it can be difficult."

"I can give it a shot."

She and I went back upstairs to the phone, where I gave her the number from my guide book and squirmed while she tried, in a French worse than mine, to put a hold on two beds for us. Finally, she switched to English, which the person on the other end apparently understood just fine.

"They are full tomorrow night and the night after," she said, smiling.

With that familiar feeling of failure tightening in my chest, I went downstairs to lay out the bad news for Colin. But when I opened the door, I found him stretched ridiculously across one of the dainty twin beds, sound asleep.

I lay down on the other bed, unable to sleep. I ran through our options in my head. There were a few to consider. From Landry, the route split in three directions, the variants all meeting up again after a few days, about sixty miles to the south. One route stayed low and wound through a handful of small villages. The towns looked charming, but the walking looked boring, too easy, and I didn't want Colin to think he'd wasted his time. The second way went up into the mountains but followed such a convoluted path that it added several days to the journey. The third option was the best. It was short and difficult and, with any luck, exciting—three or four days in the high mountains with once-in-a-lifetime views and some of the most isolated huts on the whole route. This was the way I wanted to go, the hard way. But for now, that didn't really matter, since all three routes went to the same place after Landry, and we still needed a place to sleep.

The sun was beginning to set, so I woke Colin and we asked about dinner. Since we were the only guests that night, dinner wasn't being served and we were given the name of a restaurant down the road.

The place was empty except for an old woman washing dishes at a bar, who, judging from the puzzled look on her face, did not understand what we were doing there. With no common language between us, the conversation relied almost entirely on pointing. I pointed to my mouth, Colin pointed to his stomach, I pointed to my watch. We both made palms-up question gestures. After a lot of pointing and gesturing, and, if I remember right, a sketch of a clock, we were made to understand that dinner wasn't being served yet—not for another half an hour. Of all the baffling things about eating in Europe, dining times might be the most inscrutable. It isn't that Europeans eat early or late, it's that they're so inflexible. God forbid you get hungry between lunch and dinner. When we returned thirty minutes later, we were still the only patrons, but the woman seated us immediately and brought out menus.

Over pizza, as calmly as I could, I explained the many issues that were throwing wrenches in my not-at-all-well-thought-out plan for the next few days. I wanted to go up into the high mountains, I said, but we had nowhere to sleep the next night (or any night after) and accommodation was sparse. The best I could come up with was an itinerary, which I had cobbled together that afternoon, that had us walking only a few hours a day for two days, then for about ten hours on the third day, and eight or so for the last. It was weird, but it would work, assuming there were beds free at the four huts I circled on the map. We could contact them today and make reservations in French or English or both.

"Or," I said, "we can just hit the road and hope for the best."

"What happens if we show up somewhere and they're full? Can't we just walk to the next place?"

"We could. Except sometimes the next place is six hours away."

"So what would we do?"

"Well, I have a tent, but it's really only big enough for one person."

"I didn't bring a tent."

"You probably won't need one."

"But I might?"

"You won't."

"Right. So let's call and see if we can make some reservations?"

The next place on my map was full the next night as well, but they had two beds for the night after. We put our names down. The last thing I wanted was to spend yet another day in Landry, but I figured I could use the rest. Plus, we didn't really have a choice.

With an extra day to waste before we could start, we took a bus into Bourg St. Maurice the next morning and killed a few hours there buying supplies (soap, bread, saucisson) and sipping coffee. We were both anxious to start walking, Colin especially since he hadn't done much of anything in the last few days except travel from one French city to progressively smaller ones. The mountains were calling.

We ate breakfast the next morning with Monika, the only other guest at the hotel and probably all of Landry. Monika was Swiss, from the German-speaking part of the country. She was in her mid-forties, sporting spiky black hair and a wonderfully German (Swiss-German, I suppose) accent. She was in good shape from regular walks in the Swiss and Austrian Alps. And from skiing and running. She was following a route that was a composite of several popular trails, but on the whole it wasn't terribly well known. She'd gotten lost several times, but from Landry she would be following the main route—our route—to Briançon a few days away. Her work, something having to do with cement, allowed for two weeks of holiday and she was spending them in the mountains. We compared itineraries (hers was, of course, planned and booked from top to bottom). Monika would be staying in Landry for the night but leaving the next day in the same general direction as we. Since we were only doing a half day's walk, and there were only so many places to go, we figured on seeing her again.

Outside, Colin shouldered his pack and I went over it as if it were a parachute, checking to make sure we were good to go. Water, check. Sunglasses, check. Sunscreen, check.

"Ready?" I said.

"Let's do this," Colin smiled.

"Say good-bye to Landry, because we're not coming back."

"Unless we get turned away wherever we're going."

"Right, well, hopefully that doesn't happen. And anyway, we can sleep outside."

"You can. I don't have a tent."

"So you'll sleep out in the open. Like Patrick Leigh Fermor."

"You can sleep outside. I'll use the tent."

The track led out of the hotel and up a set of stone stairs toward the church. At the top of the stairs, it split left and wound its way up into the forest. Feeling stiff from a few days off and not wanting to push Colin too hard, we moved slowly in the cool early-morning air. A day off and I'd already forgotten how awful climbing in the morning could be. We hardly spoke, but that was mostly because we were so short of breath we couldn't have gotten words out if we had wanted to.

The path cut through a long snake of smooth, paved roads that led up into the mountains and probably all the way to Nice (only a few tantalizing hours away by car). According to the book, the route from Landry was the easier of two possible paths we could have taken, "suiting walkers who arrive by train to complete this stage." I pointed this out to Colin, who was breathing heavily and sweating a lot.

"Don't worry," I said, "it gets easier."

I double-checked the guide for directions.

"'Walk up a track through the woods, crossing a stream and the road again at Pont de Chardonnet, at 870 meters.' Does that sound right?"

"I think we crossed a stream a while back."

I read on: "'Continue up the higher stretch of road. Turn right, but leave the road at the next hairpin turn.' Do you remember a hairpin turn?"

"They all feel like hairpin turns. Have you been following directions like this the whole time?"

"They sound more confusing when you read them out loud. 'Follow a track to the right, but almost immediately climb a path to the left and keep climbing. The path is later barred, so turn left and climb steeply to the road again. Turn right to follow it, then later right again to follow a clear track.' Usually there are signs pointing the way, and little red-and-white markers painted on rocks and trees, but I haven't seen one in a while."

"I'm sure we're on the right track. Let's just keep moving. I'll keep my eyes open for signs."

An hour later, we saw a sign for Moulin and another for Palais de la Mine, which, to my relief, at least sounded familiar. The last thing I wanted to do was get us lost on Colin's first day. The problem, I'll admit, was that somewhere in the back of my head, I wasn't convinced he really wanted to be there. I had no basis for this feeling other than my own insecurities about leading a good friend on what could turn out to be a misguided, painful week of walking. But I suspected he had agreed to join me early on, before he had had time to really think it through, then changed his mind but didn't want to back out. The least I could do was keep us on the right path.

Higher up, we came to an abandoned building that I identified, with the help of a very large sign, as the Palais de la Mine, the former headquarters of a large silver and lead mining operation in the region. The palace had seen better days: the paint was faded and blotched with light spots where it looked as if it had been splashed with bleach, the corrugated metal roof was rusted, and the whole structure looked like it might be brought down at any moment by a strong gust of wind.

"We're on the right track," I said, offering Colin the corresponding page of the book as proof that we weren't lost.

"I know. I saw some markers a while back."

"You might have said something."

"I figured you saw them."

"How do you feel?"

"Great. My legs are burning a little, but it's not nearly as hard as you made it sound."

"Well, today is kind of an easy day. It will get harder."

"I don't mind if it doesn't get harder. It's beautiful out here."

"Right, but it will get harder. Today is practically a day off, really."

"You sound like you want it to get harder."

"I want it to be exciting. You came all the way out here."

"I'm excited."

"Good. Me too."

"Good."

A bit farther up the road, we found our lodgings for the night—a small barn off a main road with a faded price menu tacked to the door. Unfortunately, but not at all surprisingly, no one was around to let us in. Then again, it was early. I had heard that at some of the smaller huts the staff won't arrive until late in the afternoon, or sometimes not at all, unless they are sure someone is coming. Even though we had booked ahead, it was possible that they figured the odds of two Americans actually showing up were pretty low. I suggested we wait for a while and see what would happen. We dropped our bags and spread ourselves out on the soft grass. I pulled a saucisson from my bag and cut thin slices for us with my pocket knife.

An hour later, no one had shown up and it started to look unlikely that anyone would. And despite the paper-thin slices of dry salami we were eating, we were hungry. I walked to a buvette a few minutes up the road and asked a waiter if they were serving lunch.

"I'm sorry. Eating here is impossible today."

"You are closed?"

"No, we have no space."

I looked around. All the tables were empty except one, where a waiter was smoking a cigarette with his feet up on a chair.

"But there is no one here."

"I'm sorry. It is impossible."

"I see. Well, do you know when the gîte will be opening?" I pointed back to the barn.

"This gîte is closed.

"Today?"

"Forever."

I walked back and told Colin that we probably wouldn't be sleeping in the hut that night since it was closed forever.

"So what do we do?"

I checked the book. There was another refuge about half an hour away, I explained, where we could most likely eat lunch. But I had called to get a bed the day before and they were all booked up.

"We can ask there if they have any suggestions for accommodation. Plus," I said, showing Colin the book, "it says here that bearded vultures nest nearby. So that's something."

We kept our eyes on the empty buvette as we passed, and I made eye contact with the cigarette-smoking waiter. "Don't even think of eating there," I said to Colin. "It's impossible."

Luckily, lunch was easily procured at the next refuge, and we gorged on omelettes and bread like we had spent the last three days in the woods foraging for mushrooms and scraping the meat of squirrel ribs with our teeth. Stuffed, we pulled the book out like the holy object it had become. I opened it to a map of the area.

"Here," I said, pointing at the page. "It's a long walk, maybe six hours from here and sort of off-route, but it's a possibility."

"What about here?" Colin said, fingering another hut even farther away.

"Yeah, we could, but I'm afraid we wouldn't make it there before dark."

"There's also this one, but I think I called them, and they were booked all week. I can't be sure though. I called a bunch of them. Let me see if I can borrow a phone."

Inside, a pristine dining room gleamed in the noon light.

"*Excuse moi, pouvez je faire le telephone,*" I said to the woman behind the counter, slamming French words together like train cars without breaks.

"You want the telephone?"

"Yes, please."

"Who do you call?"

"I need to call a refuge to see if we can stay for tonight."

"Why you don't stay here?"

"It's full. I called yesterday."

"We have room. There is only one other man here tonight."

"I'm sure I called and was told it was full. Are you certain?"

"Of course. I don't know who you called, but it was not someone here."

The one other man was called Herbie. He was old and English and spoke with an accent so hard to understand I had to have him repeat what he said multiple times before I could get enough to respond. The three of us dined alone on soup, pasta, and cake in the middle of the large main hall. Colin and I had spent the afternoon basking in our good fortune and exploring the area around the refuge. We had lain on van-sized boulders in the sun and listened to the whine of flies and the occasional peal of a kid's laughter somewhere off in the distance. About a mile away, athletic French people climbed a sheer rock wall for fun. When I noticed a trail of little brown ants with outsized pincers making their way to my pack, I left Colin and walked back to the relative safety of the refuge's deck to read, which is where I first met Herbie, who was, like the man in the hood, nervously jotting notes in the smallest notebook I've ever seen. What were they writing, I wondered? I'd seen dozens of note takers along the way. Were they noticing things I wasn't? I'd have given a lot to read Herbie's diary—to read anyone's walking diary—but I never got the chance.

Herbie had been walking in the mountains for at least twenty-five years and treated the subject with very little preciousness. It was simply something he did and had always done, always alone, and always in France. He did not speak French—"just enough to get by." He'd been on this very route, he said, half a dozen times. Walked it backwards and forwards. He was wiry and slight, on the short side, and wore glasses perched on a large nose that made him look more like a fuddy-duddy old train station attendant than an experienced mountain walker. I don't know what he did back in London; he never spoke about it. In fact, he never really spoke. Rather, he chirped declarations that sometimes related to the conversation going on around him, but just as often didn't.

Remarkably, Herbie had been in Landry at the same time as we, though in the course of our conversation we never figured out where he had stayed. As far as I knew, there was only one hotel in town. I like to picture him talking to himself in a clearing somewhere in the woods. After dinner, we went up to the dormitory where Herbie squeaked a quick goodnight and fell asleep fully clothed with all the lights on.

When I woke up the next morning, Herbie was already gone. It was seven o'clock, which meant the sun was just barely out. Maybe he knew the way well enough to do it in the dark. After a quick breakfast, Colin and I left feeling very good, since, for the first time, accommodation wouldn't be an issue as it was already booked for today. In a fit of phone calls the night before, I booked a few places for the next few days. I'm sure I double booked some days with the intention of calling to cancel if the reservation didn't work out. It felt like the safest thing to do.

12

There is an illusory quality to being in the mountains in the early morning when the air is cool and the light diffuse. It's as if part of you were still asleep and dreaming. You have to keep reminding yourself that it's real. At the same time, you know it can't last. The sun will come up, and sweat will start to trickle down your forehead. You'll get hungry, or thirsty, or achy—or, more likely, all three at once. But that morning was perfect and quiet and gauzy.

We glided through larch woods until the path spilled onto a large *alpage,* a high-altitude meadow. A narrow stream wound through the valley in swooping esses perfect enough to be an Andy Goldsworthy installation. Small waterfalls fell down the sides of the mountains on either side of us. I looked back at Colin to make sure he was getting all of this. He gave me a thumbs up. We climbed until a herd of cows below us coalesced into a mass of unmoving brown and black dots.

At a fork in the road, we followed a sign pointing to the Col du Palet, a high pass at eight thousand feet. Had it not been for the heavy clouds gathering to the south, the day really would have been perfect, but I could tell Colin had his eyes on the weather. I told him not to worry, which is about all you can do when it comes to weather. He said he wasn't worried, and I said it looked like the storm was moving fast enough that it would cross the route before we got that far south, a prediction that was based on nothing. In fact, I'm awful at reading the weather. A few days earlier, a woman sitting next to me at breakfast warned about coming rain like a fortune teller. With absolute certainty, she said rain would fall the next day. The skies were perfectly clear, and I asked how she was so sure. The birds, she said. "The birds are flying low. They do that because the insects are flying low. The pressure pushes them all lower. The clouds are coming." I told her if it rained that day I would eat my shoe. Of course, it poured.

We reached the refuge a little after one (still relatively early), by which point even I could tell that the clouds were about to dump rain all over us. A cold wind blew up the mountain and pushed us inside the hut, where we put on our warmer clothes, sipped hot tea, and assumed the look of bored children stuck inside on a rainy day. With the storm picking up steadily outside, we leafed mindlessly through old French magazines that neither of us could read, had short conversations every few minutes about nothing at all, and stared out the window hoping for a break in the weather. In the hut with us was a family with actual children—one boy, age six or seven, and a baby, who looked much happier than we did. They were on vacation and traveling with a pair of donkeys to haul their gear. They would go on until everyone was sick of it, the father told us. So far, it had it been great. "Walking with donkeys is the best way to walk." I told Colin to remember that for next time. Every few minutes, the beasts brayed like foghorns out front.

With six hours to go before dinner, I took out my maps and the book, but there wasn't much left to plan. Having only walked a few miles over the last couple days, our refuge options for the next few days were limited, and I'd reserved beds at all of them. For entertainment, I read the next day's description aloud to Colin:

"'Most of the day's walk is in the Parc National de la Vanoise. The heart of the national park is a wildlife haven, so keep an eye open for bouquetin, chamois, marmots, and golden eagles.'"

"Have you seen any wildlife?"

"Actually, yeah. Some chamois near Mont Blanc. And a million marmots."

"I wonder if they come out in the rain."

"The rain should be gone by tomorrow. It looks like it will blow past us overnight," I said, squinting out the window. "Listen to this: 'The geology around the Col du Palet is quite mixed. On the ascent, the underlying rock is a mixture of limestone and schist. On the col itself, both can be found, while nearby, crumbling gray humps are rich in gypsum.' It goes on: 'On the way downhill, the limestone is dolomitic and full of tiny holes.'"

"So at the very least, we will see rocks tomorrow."

"Exactly."

I turned a few more pages of a magazine with pictures of smiling French people hanging from the sides of mountains. Colin hunched over his massive camera and scrolled through the pictures he had taken. We were just about to hit rock bottom in terms of boredom when Monika walked through the door, followed by

Herbie a minute later. They were both soaked to the bone, and like the true mountain walkers they are, not the least bit bothered by it. It felt like a proper reunion, despite the fact that we had shared only two or three conversations between the four of us.

A few minutes after they arrived, one of the kitchen staff bid the hut good-bye and stepped out into the rain. From the window, we watched her climb until all we could see through the sloshing rain was the small red dot of her backpack, and then nothing at all. I asked a man in the kitchen where she was a going so late in the day.

"Home," he said. "She lives on the other side of the mountain. Her shift is finished."

I went back to the window, but she was long gone. For a split second, I caught myself wishing I lived on the other side of the mountain and was only a short walk from home. But I shook the thought off like a bad dream and joined our new friends at the table.

Colin said, "Only four hours until dinner."

13

Before I even opened my eyes, I listened for rain. Nothing. Only the soft inhaling and exhaling of the people asleep around me. The room was small, just large enough for two long rows of beds. It was five thirty. People wouldn't be waking up for another hour. I climbed out of my sleeping bag, put on a sweatshirt, and went outside. It was still nearly pitch dark, with only enough light to see the outlines of the mountains, the two donkeys tied to the post, and out of the corner of my eye, the distinctly avian facial features of Herbie, who was standing about ten feet away. He had been outside for god knows how long. Clouds were coming up from below us in soft gray wisps.

"Bloody cold, innit?"

"Freezing. What are you doing out here?"

"Nothin' like an early morning."

"How long have you been awake?"

"I don't know to be honest. I'm going back to bed though."

The four of us had breakfast together and compared plans. Herbie was going off in a direction no one could quite pinpoint on a map. But he insisted he'd done it before and it was beautiful. Plus, he said, he always carried a sleeping bag that closed up around his head, too—which sounded more like a body bag to me—in case he got stranded away from shelter. ("Only had to use it a few times, too.") Monika was headed one refuge past us. Ours looked to be about five hours away, which was almost a full day of walking. As long as the weather held—which it did not look like it would do—we would be fine.

There was a twisted quality to the scenery that morning, as if the land had been wrung out and warped by the storm. The lines sloped and climbed around corners and soft turns. It was mesmerizing to move through; I couldn't take my eyes off the ground around me. It was like walking through one of Thomas Hart Benton's rubbery murals. Ahead of me, Colin stopped and waited a few minutes to show off a heap of rocks that looked like a thousand melted candles.

"Must be the famous humps rich in gypsum?" he said.

We caught up with Monika about an hour from the refuge near the Croix de Longan, which sits on a hill at 7,500 feet. She was calmly layering herself in all sorts of water- and weatherproof gear that she pulled out of her bag like a magician with colored ribbons.

"Do you think it's going to rain?" Colin asked.

"Well," she said, looking at the awful mass of storm clouds mounting to the east, "it seems likely, I think so, yes."

Other than expensive jackets that did an admirable job of keeping the rain out and cheap covers for our bags that mostly redirected the water to the bottom of my pack where my sleeping bag soaked it up, Colin and I were pitifully defenseless against a storm as large as the one we were looking at. I couldn't imagine Monika's gear would help much, either, but I still wished I hadn't skimped on those items when I was buying my equipment. The three of us walked together until we reached Val Claret, a bizarrely developed resort town dropped in the middle of the mountains. Herbie had warned us about Val Claret—"bloody ugly place"—and he was not wrong. The city, if you could call it that, sat in a depression surrounded by mountains on all sides. To the west, the mountains held very little grass and looked to be made entirely of gravel. From where we stood, above the empty brown high-rises, the whole scene had the manufactured feel of a city in some shoddy North Korean propaganda film. I mentioned this to Monika, who said she had actually been to North Korea and agreed—it did not look real.

At a fork on the north side of the city, the path split. Monika insisted on going right, which she was convinced was the faster way. I was certain, having studied the maps, that there was a shortcut to the left. So we split up. Through increasingly damp air, Colin and I climbed through fields riven with small bike paths and signs marking ski *pistes*. When the town was no longer visible behind us, we took a quick break to put our phones in plastic zip bags before the real rain started. Burying my phone meant that I would have no photographs until we were on the other side of the storm or inside the hut. The problem, which is worth mentioning, is that there would be a stretch of the walk of which I would have no photographic record. Normally, I took pictures every half hour or so—pictures of nothing, really—pictures of the sky, the path, the trees. Or pictures of small details, some piece of nature that looked out of place, or that I wanted to remind myself to look up later. In a way, my memories of the walk run the risk of being supplanted by memories of looking at my own photographs, whether on my phone at the end of a day, or on my laptop in the months since. I think this happens to everyone. It's impossible to tell at this point what I remember directly and what I remember indirectly, from a picture.

Photographs are odd like that. They've shaped, and continue to shape, my experience after the fact. But they're not entirely reliable. A camera's shutter is only open for a fraction of a second—and the sharper the image, the less time has actually been captured. If I have a thousand pictures, and each one represents one one-thousandth of a second, I've only committed one single second to digital memory. It's up to my brain to fill in the blanks. But I did not take pictures to capture the jaw-dropping beauty of the mountains. The camera in my phone is too shitty for that, for one thing, and the beauty can't be captured anyway. I took pictures—thousands of them, in fact—to act as little breadcrumbs, creating a digital trail that I could trace my way through in ten or twenty or fifty years. All I can do is hope that when my mind is dull, my pictures, which I guard like precious jewels, will still be sharp as they tell this story—or some version of it anyway.

The point is, I don't remember this particular section in quite the same way as I remember the rest; it's somehow sharper, lit by staccato stabs of lightning. When the rain started falling, we were completely exposed on a nearly flat valley above eight thousand feet. A little higher up, snow stays on the ground all year. With no gloves, our hands froze in grips around our walking poles. I put my right fist in a pocket for a few minutes and carried a pole under my arm. I switched when the other hand became too cold. We moved swiftly, our eyes locked on the ground. A line of light split the air and touched down two or three hundred feet to our right. I saw the smoke that was left after the electricity had dispersed.

The thunder rattled our bones. I remember feeling nervous, genuinely afraid the lightning would strike near enough to fry us. We were standing in water and covered in it. After the third or fourth bright flash, the weight of our bags lifted and we both started to run. There was no shelter, just an open valley covered in large rocks. The ground dipped and shifted under us. We stayed close to it, moving like criminals; our feet barely touched the ground. We flew through the storm as if we could dodge the falling drops of rain.

The sky had gone gray and green, the color of putrid smoke. We lost track of time. We slipped on rocks. I may have fallen at one point, but I can't be sure. Our feet sunk into the ground until the waterproofing on our shoes simply gave up. By now, our hands were so cold we couldn't warm them up, so we let them freeze until they were pink and numb. It didn't take long. The hood on my rain jacket made it impossible to see anything in my periphery, so I focused on the ground and on Colin. Every time lightning hit, our valley went from ochre to black to translucent. And the sharp crack of lightning was always followed by a deep, deafening report of thunder. Below us, deep in the valley (by now we were high up on the lip), a perfectly round pool of white ice glimmered through the dull air. I stopped for half a second to look at it, reached for my camera out of instinct, and then remembered it was locked away deep inside my pack in a plastic bag. Today, I can still see the ice, reflecting white, but I don't trust that I remember it the way it actually was. I've changed it, made it brighter, bigger, whiter. I'm glad I don't have a picture of it; it could only disappoint.

We climbed up a col on slimy scree, using our frozen hands to steady ourselves, and slipped over the other side down to a vast grassy meadow. The path stretched out in a nearly straight brown line. We kept our pace, glad to have solid ground to move on. The lightning grew less frequent, less terrifying. Stopping to rest for a minute, Colin and I asked each other if we were okay. Breathless and charged, he looked at me and nodded. I like to think I saw excitement in his eyes, real excitement, the excitement you feel when your life has been made momentarily uncertain.

Soaked, cold, tired, and hungry, we finally spotted the refuge from a couple of miles away. Our pace quickened involuntarily until the refuge looked too close and too good to be true. It was only once we opened the door marked *accueil* and startled the three teenagers who had been left to run the place on their own that I felt any sense of relief.

Sleepily, one of the teenagers put his phone down and led us to the sleeping area, which was a separate building, and then to the toilet and showers, also separate, which were down the rock path a few meters. There was no hot water, he said.

Then he took us to the dining room, a large wooden room where we found Monika changing into dry clothes and hanging her sopping plastic rain pants on a line. The room was only marginally warmer than outside, and we stood there, shivering but elated. At least we were dry—or we would be soon. Monika had arrived a few minutes earlier and wouldn't be staying. She was only there long enough to dry some of her clothes and warm up. She would then walk another hour or two to her stop for the night.

"What about the rain?" I said.

"Yes. It is not fun," she said matter-of-factly.

"Forget not fun. What about dangerous?"

"I'll be fine," she said. And that was it. Her confidence was stunning.

With our wet clothes and soaked sleeping bags hanging down from the ceiling, the three of us sat down to tea in a dry corner and breathed a collective sigh of relief at having made it. Our nerves slowly unwound until the last few hours felt like a distant memory, a different lifetime. After half an hour or so, we heard a slight letting up in the rain and Monika repacked her gear and said good-bye. I was thrilled, personally, not to have to go back outside that day. It looked dreadful out there.

"Good luck," Colin said.

Sipping bottomless cups of hot tea, some lines from a Jack Gilbert poem about rain crept out from a corner of my brain and bounced around my skull.

Joy has been a habit. Now suddenly this rain. Joy has been a habit. Now suddenly this rain.

There was much more to the poem, but I couldn't remember the rest. I had read it earlier that year in a van while crossing from Kosovo into Albania in a torrential downpour (the storm ended up cutting the electricity for most of the night once I arrived in Tirana). The vehicle sloshed and skidded like a drunk on ice. Inside the van was a young girl going to a brother's or uncle's or cousin's wedding (we had waited over two hours for her to finish getting ready); a family with two young children who vomited into plastic bags every few minutes (the bags were then tossed out the window of the van); and an older man who lived in Germany. The man was on his way home to see his mother, who was in her nineties. He had been traveling for three days, he said. It was dark outside the van, which made it impossible to see anything through the window. (To this day, I have no idea how our driver managed to deliver us safely.) When a spike of lightning landed, the mountains lit up just long enough for me to be able to make out the serrated outline of the peaks, jagged and sharp and wild like the mangled teeth inside a shark's mouth. "In Albania," the man said to me, "we say these mountains are cursed." Albania, I had heard, is famous for its treacherously poor roads, but I hadn't heard of its cursed mountains. He was referring, I found out later, to the actual name of the range, which translates to "accursed mountains." They are a part of the larger Dinaric Alps, which run up the Balkan peninsula and touch, ever so gently and many miles to the east, the Alps I was currently walking through. As the man fell asleep next to me, I went back to my book and found the words that were now rolling through my cold, wet head many months later:

Suddenly this defeat. That was the first line, I remembered. Suddenly this defeat. Joy has been a habit. Now suddenly this rain.

A few minutes after Monika left, the door swung open and in bounded two ballet-lithe young men in full neoprene bodysuits. They said something in French to each other and then to us, which neither Colin nor I understood.

"I'm sorry?" Colin said.

"Ah, English. It's freezing in here."

"I know."

"Why don't you use the stove?"

"What stove?"

He pointed to a giant metal box in the opposite corner of the room that, once it had been pointed out, was obviously a stove.

"I didn't see it," I said. The two of them made quick work of the wood, which we hadn't noticed either, while Colin and I looked on like children. It was only once the room started to warm up that I realized how cold I had been. I felt my skin tingle, my muscles start to melt. The two men stood over the box with their arms extended toward it and bounced like boxers from one foot to the other.

"You are English?"

"American."

"You are very far from home. Are you lost?"

"I hope not," I said. "I'm walking to Nice and my friend is joining me from Landry to Modane."

"We came from Landry today and will go to Modane tomorrow."

"That's, like, seventy-five miles. How can you do that in two days?"

"We are runners. My friend is training for a competition."

I was busy doing the math in my head that might make that distance even remotely possible when the door swung open again. The family with the donkey from the night before rushed in from the rain, which the wind sent spitting into the room, and slammed the door behind them. Suddenly, our quiet room became incredibly loud. The father was shouting at the mother, who was shouting back at the father. The boy was standing very still, dripping water into a puddle at his feet. The baby, bright pink and looking dangerously hypothermic, was howling at what had to have been her top volume. I had never heard a baby scream so loudly; it was the gold standard of baby volume.

The family worked at rapidly stripping to their underwear, like people do in movies when they are dragged out of an icy lake, and hanging their clothes, crowding the ceiling space with their dripping gear. The boy waited naked until his father threw him a bundle of dry clothes. The mother tried frantically to warm the baby by the fire, rubbing and kneading it into the soft flesh of her own body. One of the runners, who turned out to be a doctor, sprang into action, pulling a blanket from his bag and wrapping the baby in it. Hot kettles of tea were boiled. The baby screamed its little head off.

Colin and I watched all of this rather helplessly but not without a great deal of sympathy—we were cold, too, after all. The baby looked miserable, far more miserable than I could ever remember myself being; the boy only slightly less so. Slowly, the action settled down a bit. Everyone moved toward the stove like moths to a flame, and I went back to trying to figure out how it was possible to run in two days what was taking me and Colin six. And if that was just the training, what was the competition?

Over dinner—and the still-piercing cries of the freezing baby—I asked the doctor what it was like to cover so much ground so quickly. Was it dangerous? How does one eat for such a run? Why would anyone ever do it? I'd heard of ultramarathons, events of fifty or a hundred miles, but not of long-distance mountain running, which seemed idiotically dangerous, at least to me. The answers I got were vague at best, which led me to believe that, like myself and the walk I was on, one's motives are not always that easily articulated. There are events, one of them told me, that last for days. Some runners—the best ones—can go without sleep for the entire race.

"By the end, they are delirious," the doctor said. "Beyond exhausted, but it is not impossible. Humans can train their bodies for so many things. We cannot imagine our limits. I can run twenty-five miles in a day, and then wake up and do the same tomorrow. It will be very difficult, especially in the mountains. But I know I can do this, because I have done it before, many times. What I don't know is how many days I could repeat this. Maybe only two. Maybe ten. The excitement is in coming close to your limit. The satisfaction is not like anything else."

Just then, in what I imagine was an instinctual effort to warm her tiny body, the baby reached out and touched the glowing stove. In my memory, I hear the heart-wrenching sound of skin searing, but I know it didn't happen like that. I know I heard nothing at all until the room filled instantaneously with the child's breathless, desperate, ear-splitting wail. It was the most dispiriting, disheartening, depressing sound in the world, and it went on for a very long time until our faces hung like the worn faces of soldiers who had just lost one of their men. The baby carried on well past dinner, past dessert, and through a round of weird alcoholic shots, offered without explanation from one of the teenagers, which turned out to be coconut-flavored rum, perhaps the last drink one would expect to find high up in the mountains of France. It tasted terrible, since it was probably homemade, but it burned and it warmed.

"Glad you came?" I asked Colin.

"Very," he said.

I couldn't tell if he was serious, but after a few more shots I didn't care. I felt warm and muddy, drowsy enough to sleep. I stumbled off to the bed, climbed into my sleeping bag, closed it over my head, and passed out. Sometime in the middle of the night, I woke up and listened not to the child's crying but to the soft whimpering and steady breathing of the whole family. And to Colin, too. Our bodies burned like furnaces in the cold air of that dark, unheated room, and we warmed ourselves and each other, cocooned there in our sleeping bags somewhere on the side of a mountain, a world away from another living thing.

No one had the weather forecast the next morning. One of the teenagers said it would probably rain and another said that it would probably rain a lot. The light at the end of that cold, wet tunnel, though, was, assuming we didn't slip off a mountain or get struck by lightning, we would be sleeping in real beds in a proper hotel in a genuine town at the end of the day. But that was still many miles and many, many steps away.

We left early, irrationally hoping to walk ahead of the rain, which, based on the last two days, seemed heaviest in the afternoon. The runners were either still asleep or already gone, and the poor family was strapping things to their donkeys as we prepared to leave. They had decided to cut their journey short and head back the other way. I didn't quite get the logic in this since there was a town not too far south, and moving backwards would mean at least two more days in the high mountains. Also, I couldn't imagine walking yesterday's stony, frozen gauntlet again, but the family was firm in their decision. The donkeys let out a disgusting noise, and with that, we said good-bye and started walking.

According to the book, the route we were on has been popular since the Bronze Age. It also notes that the traverse is "wonderfully scenic." Historic or scenic, I just hoped it was easy. And it was, climbing gently enough in parts that we didn't really notice an incline and staying flat for long misty stretches through a light rain. It was paradise compared to the day before. We stopped several times to take pictures of the clouds wrapping around the peaks like winter scarves and the shiny streams bubbling over rocks. The views, unfortunately, were not as wonderfully scenic and certainly not what I had promised when I pitched the walk to Colin. But priorities had changed, and we felt lucky enough to be relatively dry.

At least until the real rain. It finally started around nine, just as we rounded a corner and spotted two figures high up on the mountain to our right—the runners. They were probably an hour ahead of us, but it is difficult to judge distances in the mountains. I could just barely make out the trail in front of us. At one point, the ground was so wet the path disappeared completely—it just dissolved back into the earth, like a healed scar. We walked in a general southernly direction using a system of cairns that had been built by other walkers as a rough guide. But sometimes those disappeared as well, and we relied on nothing but luck. Often it was hard to tell if luck was even on our side.

Needless to say, when we did start climbing, it was hard. The path was steep and the ground wet; it was like walking on ice— only uphill and on loose rocks. Each step had to be taken cautiously, with one's weight perfectly balanced. If you weren't careful, one leg would shoot out to the side or backwards and send all your muscles scrambling to correct the tilt. Slowly, we picked our way up until the trail leveled off and followed a stream to a bed of small lakes.

The path rolled straight into one of the larger of the lakes, where a bridge of heavy flat stones stretched out before us into the fog. The end was somewhere ahead, but it was impossible to tell how far. I was also not entirely sure this was the right way, having quietly lost track of the markings a while back. I did not mention this to Colin, since I was sure it would only alarm him and make him regret this week of his life even more. I started to cross, keeping my eyes on the farthest stone I could see, which materialized again with each step. Three or four—or ten or fifteen—stones in I could see neither the end nor the beginning. I paused for a moment and looked back. When I started moving again, a man appeared on the other side walking toward me. We passed each other in silence, not even a nod. But the sight of another walker was enough to calm us.

We dried off and warmed up over tea inside a refuge at well over eight thousand feet (the highest on the route, according to the book). The clouds were so thick around the building that the windows were pure white.

"Good tea," I said.

"Excellent."

"Think of it this way: anyone can go hiking in great weather. Your experience—our experience—is far more rare. And more interesting, I think."

"In that case," he laughed, "I can't complain. It is unlikely I will ever spend so much time cold and wet in the Alps again. I doubt I'll ever forget it."

"Anyway, you have a few more days. This rain can't go on forever."

"I'm happy to be here," he said with heartbreaking sincerity. And I was happy to have him there, thrilled to share these mountains with an old friend.

Back outside, the dreamy white clouds had turned gray and sodden. The ground was muddy, and our gear was heavy with moisture. The track descended sharply, dropping 1,600 feet in about an hour. At 6,500 feet, we stopped again to warm up in another refuge. I took out the maps. We were only an hour from the town, but it was proving impossible to leave the shelter of the refuge. The dining room had been done up like a hunting lodge from the 1970s: lots of dark, polished wood, soft and worn seats, the thick smell of stewing meat and warm bread. The bartender cleaned glasses while the waitress sat at the window and stared outside. It took two beers each (maybe three) to work up the energy to walk outside into the pouring rain again.

An hour and a half later and fifteen hundred feet closer to sea level, we spilled out of a dank woods on the eastern edge of Pralognan-la-Vanoise, a popular ski town of a thousand people. At the tourism office, a kind lady who didn't really understand why we didn't have a reservation for a hotel directed us to one a few minutes away.

"It's a busy season, though," she warned. "They may not have any rooms."

"Is there another hotel if they don't?"

"Yes, but I believe everything is full tonight."

"I've heard that before," I said.

"Good luck."

"I've heard that, too."

We ran to the hotel like our lives depended on it. There was exactly one room left and we moved into it like conquerors. We hung our wet clothes, emptied our wet bags, and threw our gear around until the floor was strewn with the random odds and ends that somehow bring a walker's pack to a backbreaking weight: fingernail clippers, sunglasses, a few shirts, a sleeping bag, a jar of peanut butter, a knife. We took turns taking shamefully long showers in scalding hot water in the room's expansive bathroom. I used as much soap and shampoo as I could; I don't think I've ever been cleaner in my life.

"Now," I said, "Let's check out this town."

"I need to buy some rain gear."

"That is a very good idea. But I don't think it will rain anymore. Still, you're probably right. We should buy some better rain gear. Gloves at least."

After we nabbed the hotel room, our luck just kept getting better. The center of the town was essentially a collection of ski shops, sport shops, and outdoor outfitters, one after another. We could not have hoped for a better place to land for the day. At one of the shops, a clerk warned that snow was likely up in the mountains for the next few days. I did not pass this on to Colin.

I did, however, buy a lot of expensive accessories in preparation for the worst: waterproof gloves, pants, a warmer shirt, thicker socks, and a new rain cover for my bag that I hoped would do more than simply direct the rain into my sleeping bag. Colin went for gloves and pants. We both felt much better about our prospects for the next day; plus, we were each a couple hundred euros lighter.

14

Looming large the next morning was something I had read in the book the night before: "Broken quartzite forms a boulder-scree, then more schist proves loose on the final steep climb to a col. The far side of the col is steep and stony, but less likely to carry large snow patches." The col was the Col de Chavière. Scraping 9,500 feet, it is the highest point on the route. In good weather, the views are supposed to be absolutely breathtaking, stretching all the way back to Mont Blanc and ahead to Monte Viso, a peak many miles away on the Italian side of the border. In bad weather, it sounded like a nightmare. It sounded like certain death.

Again, I chose not to mention this to Colin. I did consider offering the idea of staying another day in town, but the forecast didn't look any better for the next few days; it actually looked worse the next day. There would be no escaping this, I thought.

The best I could do was hope for a spell of clear weather when we got there.

The difference in temperature between eight thousand feet above sea level and five thousand is significant enough that the morning air, when we left the hotel, felt balmy. Backtracking through the village and back up into the forest from which we had emerged the day before, we managed to get lost pretty quickly. We were looking for the trail, but the signage was confusing, the trees obscured any straight view, and the path sloped confusingly downhill for a while when it should have gone up. Frustrated and confused, we walked back up—that is, in the wrong direction—and tried to retrace our steps to find a more logical route. I checked the maps and the book, but neither was helpful. Finally, Colin, who is far more level-headed than I am, spotted a small red-and-white marker on a dirty tree trunk, and having only wasted forty-five minutes, we righted ourselves.

Above the trees, the path widened and rolled resplendently over high green hills. Soft white clouds hung low in the sky, but for the most part they held their rain. Still, every few minutes my brain flashed to a picture of a bleak, wind-battered peak four thousand feet up, dark with loose schist and covered in boulder scree, like something out of the scarier parts of *The Lord of the Rings* movies.

Without the rain, Colin was able to stop every few minutes for a picture. The low, creamy clouds moving around us, the light-brown cows that crossed and recrossed the path, and endless valleys—it all begged to be photographed. And Colin, who is a professional photographer, was happy to snap away as we made very slow upward progress toward the col, completely oblivious to what lay ahead.

Five hours after we started walking, we still hadn't reached our midway point, a refuge and restaurant that was only supposed to be four (relatively easy) hours from Pralognan. This was not an optimal pace, but I couldn't bring myself to deny Colin his pictures. He'd lugged a heavy camera bag and an assortment of lenses all the way from New York. Whenever it rained, he had to pack it in a large trash bag that would then have to be buried safely in the center of his pack. To take it out and put it away was a major undertaking.

We found the refuge a few minutes off-route up in the high mountains at around eight thousand feet. It was built on a hill and constructed from wood and stone, roughly in the shape of a half circle. Large solar panels tilted up toward the sun on the flat side. The structure was supported by a series of stilts. Windows lined the rounded side. It looked like a spacecraft that had fallen into the mountains and converted to a hotel.

Inside was an eerily modern and almost futuristic dining room and kitchen, empty except for the staff—hearty, mountaineering types—and a lone middle-aged man with fair skin and a copy of the very same guide I was using (the only other copy I've ever seen since). As we ate (omelettes again), the clouds closed in on the refuge and obscured any view we might have had. Colin pointed out that the fog was following us, and I couldn't argue.

Even now, in Belgrade, where I've returned to and where I'm writing this, a late-November fog settles sometime early in the morning or late at night every day and whites out my windows. Walking around outside, I can see five, maybe ten feet ahead. I like wandering around in it, though, with thoughts of the mountains fading in and out. It's like a screen onto which I can project whatever I want. I walk from one end of my neighborhood to the other, past the cafés and bakeries and grocery stores, to Kalemegdan Park, where the Danube meets the Sava on its way to the Black Sea. I stroll the length of Kneza Mihaila with its ornate old buildings and down to a small park by the Palace Hotel. Belgrade, like so many once-great cities, is especially beautiful blanketed by fog. I can do this for hours on end, walk around in the clouds, until my feet are sore, trying to remember the smallest, least important details of the Alps until I'm not sure anymore if they are real or if I'm making them up. When the clouds burn off, I walk back to my apartment and write down as many fragments as I can before they fly out of my head.

In the refuge, Colin and I ate our omelettes and drank our coffee, delaying going outside again, where it had gotten colder and wetter over the last half hour. On the wall behind Colin hung a large map of the mountains that covered the area from slightly north of where we were all the way to the sea. We found our location and traced the red line that extended down over the col and through a handful of towns to the Côte d'Azur.

"Going to Nice?" It was the man who had been sitting alone in the corner. He was American.

"He is," Colin said. "I'm only here for a few days."

"Doing the whole thing?" he asked me.

"I started near Geneva. I guess that's the whole thing."

"Where you from?"

"Kansas, both of us. You?"

"Indiana."

His name was Dave, and he had been walking pieces of France for years. Dave had done much of the route we were on, but never the whole thing at once. But he was doing it now, more or less. He was in his mid-fifties, thin, and red from the sun, bald on the top of his head. He spoke with a soft, almost broken voice—a midwestern voice.

"At this point," I said, "I figured I wouldn't meet any other Americans, let alone one from Indiana."

"I'm not sure Americans really know about this route, or about walking in France in general. But I don't mind. It's better that way. Fewer people, less spoiled. Even without Americans, everything from here to Nice is booked."

"Wait," I said. "What do you mean everything?"

"It's all booked up. They were all full weeks ago when I made my reservations. A few days south of here, sleeping options really thin out, and they book up fast. It's still the holiday month for the French. Did you book ahead?"

"We only have as far as tomorrow night reserved. After that, I'm counting on our good luck."

He laughed. "Well, good luck then."

Dave was going all the way to Modane that day, he said, which was still a ways to go, so he had to get going. But he would be resting there for a day. "It's a small city," he said, "so, who knows, we may see each other again. Good meeting you both."

I meant to ask him about the col in bad weather, but I was still thinking about not finding a place to sleep for the next however many days, and he was already gone, out in the clouds somewhere.

It began to rain as soon as we started to climb. We put on our new rain gear, gloves and all, and marveled at the incredible waterproofness of it. I watched the rain literally bounce off my pants. I thanked the lady at the shop for scaring me into overpaying for all of it. With the refuge below and long out of view, the ground went from thin pastures heavy with cows to large rocks that shifted and moved under our weight. We passed a spooky, flat field covered in cairns, human-built towers of stones used as landmarks, some only a few inches high, others several feet tall. It could have been a graveyard, I thought. The weather was getting worse by the minute.

Past the cairn field, the path climbed until it reached a completely barren landscape of muted gray rocks in high, soft piles. I led the way, keeping a close eye on the cairns, which marked the way when the path disappeared. At a certain point, I must have lost both because I walked up the side of a twenty-foot rock slope following what I thought were footsteps, but which were more likely depressions made by an animal. Or perhaps they were nothing at all, tricks my eyes were playing. Visibility was only a few feet in any direction. We walked along a ridge on top of the slope but it broke apart in a pit of big, sharp boulders. We backtracked. Going down the slope was much harder than coming up. We both tried a couple of times, but the ground was too loose and the hill too steep. We would have fallen straight to the bottom. After a few attempts, I said I would walk down the other side to see if the path picked up down there. I told Colin to stay where he was.

Down on the other side, I found nothing but a small patch of ice. No path. I yelled up to Colin that this wasn't the way. I didn't hear a response. I climbed back up, but there was no sign of him. I yelled again. Nothing. I felt my legs start to shake involuntarily. The book put the col at an hour from the refuge. We had been out for a little over an hour, so I knew we were close. But without being able to see, we were shooting in the dark. I walked to my left, shouted again, and then heard, as if from very far way, Colin shouting back to me. I found him a few rocky hills away and quickly picked my way up and over.

"There's no path over there," I said.

"So where is it?"

"If I knew where it was, we'd be walking on it."

"Don't get mad at me. You're the one who got us lost."

"We're not really lost. We just need to figure out where to go."

"I think that makes us lost."

"Let me get my compass."

I got my compass out of my bag, found south, and pointed with my entire arm like I was directing airport traffic: "That way."

"Are you sure? I think it's really about to rain."

"It's not about to rain. And yes, I'm sure. The compass does not lie."

We found a way back down to where I had first led us astray and maintained a perfect southbound line. But that wasn't right, either. There was clearly no path or markings, just rocks upon rocks upon rocks.

Colin was right, though, about the rain. It started to come down on us while we stood there and turned in circles trying to spot any slight difference in the ground that might mark the trail. We were the very picture of turned around. So turned around, in fact, that neither of us had any idea from which direction we had come.

"Okay," I said. "We're lost."

"Goddamnit."

"But we're close. I'm sure we're close."

"Fuck. And it's cold."

It was very cold since we were quite high up and pretty wet, which made it colder.

"I know we are supposed to climb steeply up to the col. It's in the book."

"That's fine. But I don't see any steep climb. I don't see anything at all."

We squinted into the clouds.

"There," Colin said. "What's that?" He pointed to some rocks about thirty feet away.

"I can't see anything."

"It looks like they are stacked. It could be a marker."

I looked again. "I'll go check it out. Don't move."

I walked in the direction of Colin's rocks, which were level with us. My heart skipped a beat when I got close enough to see it: a small tower of carefully placed stones, and another a few feet ahead. I shouted back to Colin that he was right and to walk toward me. When he got there I showed him the next one.

"You found it!" I said, clapping his shoulder.

We moved from one cairn to the next, quickly, to make up for lost time. We had wasted forty-five minutes being lost and were now seriously behind schedule. Then the path dead-ended at a wall that rose almost straight up out of the rocks. The path was barely visible. It looked terribly steep with very few turns that would have eased the ascent. I was sure we would both fall off the wall and roll like rag dolls a hundred feet down to the bottom where no one would find us for days (because who in their right mind hikes in this shitty weather?). I realized, too, that the scene was ominously familiar—it was exactly like the hellish visions I'd been having all day. I had seen the place where we would die, I realized with a sinking feeling in my stomach, and hadn't recognized it as a warning.

"We don't have to climb this," I said.

"What do you mean?"

"Are you sure you're sure about this?"

"About what?"

"You sure you want to climb it?"

"What else would we do?"

"I have no idea." I said. "Turn back."

"If Dave can do it, we can do it."

I offered to go first and the climb was every bit as frightening as it looked. My feet slipped with almost every step, and I yelled back to Colin to watch out where the rocks were especially loose. I moved slowly, putting too much stress on my knees to keep my legs from kicking out. Halfway up, I stopped and waited for Colin. Neither of us looked down. I don't know how long it took to climb, whether it was thirty minutes or three, but I remember taking the last step up to the col and feeling my limbs go dead for a second. Colin was right behind me.

"Jesus Christ," he said. "Look at the view."

The south side of the col was dripping in sunlight, a yellow glow falling through thinning clouds to the velvet-soft grass below.

"It's the highest point on the route," I said, pointing to a tiny plaque that had been nailed into a boulder. The plaque read: Col de Chavière—2,796 m.

"What is that in feet?" Colin asked.

"Almost ten thousand," I said, rounding up.

"God, let's get off this mountain."

I took a picture of the sign and we started the descent, which was no less difficult than the climb and only slightly less scary. Fifteen minutes later, we were on solid, flat ground. I looked at my watch—it was almost three. We were considerably behind schedule, and I was starting to worry that our refuge might give our beds away if we didn't show up in the next couple hours. I had heard of this happening from other walkers, and I didn't know how far away we were. What I could tell from the map was that we were at standing at around nine thousand feet up and that the refuge was much, much lower.

I told Colin I was going to run ahead and try to get to the refuge quickly. He should keep walking however fast he wanted. Still buzzing with adrenaline from the col, I took off jogging. The bag felt light on my back. My legs didn't hurt. Nothing hurt, actually. I barely broke a sweat running downhill, taking switchbacks like I'd spent my life training on them. Soft meadows turned into thick woods and I kept running; I barely stopped. And then the sky tilted sideways, the sun flashed in my eyes, I saw the ground swing under me, and I crash-landed on my side before I had any chance of stopping myself. My pack, which had no doubt dragged me out of the air pretty quickly, broke my fall for the most part, but my hip hurt like hell and I counted on a bruise the next day. Standing up, I switched to a quick walk and then a few minutes later went back to a jog.

I ran for nearly an hour, mostly to get to the refuge quickly, but also because I could. Even with the fall, it was like discovering a superpower. After more than two weeks of hard-to-very-hard climbing, I was, to my own great surprise, actually in good shape—better shape, probably, than at any other point in my life. I'd been so preoccupied over the last few days with the weather and with worrying about whether I'd brought a good friend halfway around the world just to walk in the rain with me that I hadn't noticed the strides my body was making. The sensation of running that easily was like being in someone else's skin. I wondered what I could do on flat ground without a forty-pound backpack and made a mental note to test myself at some point.

Through a clearing in the trees, I spotted the refuge far down the hill at the end of a long series of zigzags that looked like the final stretch in an obstacle course. I stopped to rest for a few minutes and drank half a liter of water. But when I started downhill again, everything felt wrong. My legs were stiff, my shoulders sore, and my pack bounced around dangerously on my back. My run, which had been so smooth just ten minutes earlier, became a stilted hobble and each step sent a sharp pain from my hip to my knee and back. Aching and angry, I closed the gap between myself and the hut as quickly as I could, covering the last hundred yards of freshly-paved road in considerable pain from my feet to my shoulders.

I must have looked absolutely ragged when I walked in because the proprietor took pity on me, made me a hot cup of tea, and told me to sit and relax. I told her I had run from the col because I was afraid they might give our beds away. And that my friend had come from New York. And that it had rained the whole time. I doubt she caught everything I said, but she assured me she would not have given our beds away, even if we came after dinner. No refuge would do that, she said.

Colin rocked up fifteen minutes later, his camera hanging around his neck.

"Don't worry," I said. "They didn't give our beds away."

"I wasn't worried."

"How did you get here so quickly? Did you run, too?"

"I walked. Pretty slowly I think. I didn't take very long. We were already close when you took off."

"I felt like I was running really fast. Like, run-for-your-life fast."

"How long have you been here?"

"Fifteen, twenty minutes maybe."

"Well, you shaved fifteen minutes off my time. Not bad."

15

The city of Modane—in Herbie's inimitable words, "nothin' but a bloody ugly railway stop"—was an easy walk away the next morning. It was the final stop of Colin's tour of the French Alps. From Modane he would take a train to Avignon and then to Spain, where he would spend the second half of his vacation trying to forget how uncomfortably cold and wet he had spent the first. At least that's how I imagined it. Now that Colin was leaving, the weather was absolutely perfect—cloudless and cool, Kodachrome-azure skies in every direction.

We took the trail through the woods until all of a sudden we were in a quiet neighborhood with a small stone chapel. We followed signs to a bridge and, on the other side, continued along a main street past an auto mechanic, a lamp store, and a butcher shop to get to a row of hotels. The first place we tried was completely booked, but the second, a small three-story hotel attached to a bar, had a room on the back side that looked out over the Arc river.

The city had an undeniably industrial vibe and seemed to exist largely in service to, or as a result of, its train station, which sat on the far-western edge of the city. Across the river was the Fort du Replation, an abandoned agglomeration of concrete and steel fortifications built in the late-nineteenth century to watch over the Italian border. Specifically, the French had wanted to keep a close eye on the entrance to Fréjus Rail Tunnel, built in the 1860s to connect France and Italy by way of an eight-and-a-half-mile passage bored through the mountains. The late-nineteenth century was not the most stable time for France, and whenever tensions flared along the border the tunnel seemed to the French the perfect place for the Italians to invade. The entrance is no longer used (though the rail is); now it's a tourist attraction I didn't visit for reasons I don't remember.

After dropping our stuff at the hotel, Colin and I went for a stroll from one end of the town to the other. We stopped at a little *épicerie* to buy some food. Passing by the hotel for the second or third time, we spotted our old friend Monika, who, it turned out, was staying there, as well. It was another grand reunion since we hadn't actually figured on seeing one another again. Monika had arrived the night before and would be leaving the next morning. Somehow we were all on the same schedule, a schedule that was increasingly difficult to keep track or make sense of. Not ten minutes after seeing Monika and arranging dinner plans, we crossed paths with Dave from Indiana, on his way out of the city. I was sure he was at least a day ahead of us, but there he was, leaving Modane for god knows where that late in the afternoon.

Dinner was pizza, which seemed appropriate as we were only a stone's throw from the Italian border. But it was Colin's last night, and no amount of cheese or perfectly chewy crust or cheap house wine could change that. Monika seemed especially crestfallen. I think she preferred talking to Colin, who asked far fewer questions about why she was spending her vacation walking through the mountains. After a toast to Colin and to the mountains, we went quiet for a moment.

"Did you achieve what you wanted to?" she asked him.

"I walked a lot. That's really all I came for," he said. "And to spend time with Jon."

"Ah ha. Then you have succeeded."

I cut in. "I just wish the weather would have been better."

"The weather is only part of the walking," Monika said sagely. "The entire experience could have been very different in sunshine, but you cannot say that it would have been better. I like walking in the rain. I know I will become dry once I am inside. But outside, the clouds are beautiful, the way they move. We are above the earth, apart from the ground. It's a more spiritual journey."

I could not have agreed less, but I was happy to let Monika try to pump some positive thinking into Colin's experience.

"Maybe I am drinking too much wine," she said. "I don't know. Perhaps I have had too much time to think."

"I had a great time," Colin said. "I know Jon thinks I was miserable the whole time, but I got tons of exercise, saw really pretty things, spent the night with a family traveling by donkey. I have no regrets. There is nothing you could have done about the rain. And in a couple days I'll be in Barcelona, and I will have forgotten this whole week."

I said it would be weird tomorrow, leaving alone. I hadn't walked alone since the morning I met Colin in Landry, which felt like ages ago.

"If you want to stick around for a few more days—" I said. But my offer came out halfhearted and went unanswered.

Back in the hotel lobby, we said good-bye to Monika. In our room, I searched for something meaningful to say to Colin. It meant a lot to me that he had come out to walk and that he'd been such a good sport. He had barely complained, despite obviously complaint-worthy circumstances, and the only time I think he got angry was when I got the two of us lost on that frozen rocky hellscape. But nothing came to me, and eventually I just told him I'd be leaving early and would try not to wake him up when I packed my bag. For a while afterward, I lay awake listening to the river outside our room. It sounded, in one moment, like wind—air tearing through trees—and in the next, like nothing at all—a white noise, some elusive frequency I could never hope to hold on to.

16

I was already awake when my alarm went off at six forty-five. As softly as I could, I stuffed large bags inside smaller bags, and those inside even smaller bags. I ate a quick breakfast alone, already feeling like something had been subtracted. By seven thirty I was out the door, and by eight I was lost, having followed some signs that led to an industrial parking lot. I backtracked a bit, found where I'd gone wrong, and, now on the right path, commenced a near-vertical climb through thick woods above the city. There were a few low gray clouds, but the forecast was good. The path went under a massive raised highway and I smiled to myself thinking of Herbie cursing such a monstrosity. Colin and I would have had a good laugh about that, I thought. Mimicking Herbie had become a kind of ongoing routine, something to pass the time. I turned back to Modane, took one final look, and pushed upward.

Slightly farther up, I passed a small hamlet of houses. One had a miniature, gated stone altar with Jesus on a cross, a few other figurines, and fresh flowers. A sign on the house said CARPE DIEM. Farther still, a series of concrete pillboxes with rusted metal turrets were in the process of being slowly subsumed by alpine vegetation. I wondered if they'd been used since the Second World War, if they were even used then. I thought of French soldiers, much younger than I am now, crowded inside them for weeks, peaking through slits looking for Italians and Germans. Even in relatively peaceful times such as these, there is a certain anxiety to borderlands, some bad vibration in the atmosphere. I felt it that day, walking among the ruins, and I wondered if it wasn't another sign.

I found a sign that put the night's refuge at about two hours away. Even with the climbing, it was an easy day's walk. Above the woods, the ground flattened and the views in every direction were exactly what I had so badly wanted Colin to see: endless rows of jagged, snow-streaked mountains, lush valleys, a lone climber submitting a nearby peak. These were the scenes that photographs could never come close to capturing. I took a few pictures anyway, figuring I'd send them to Colin next time I had Wi-Fi. I never sent them, but I'm looking at them now, and they're hardly more than pixelated thumbnails—blurry, flat, and tiny.

I climbed the final stony slope to the refuge at noon and immediately spotted Dave at a picnic table outside. He waved me over.

"Where's your friend?"

"Gone." I said. "He got off at Modane."

"So you're alone. Like me."

"It appears that way, doesn't it. But I seem to pick up walking partners. I don't think I've spent more than three days completely alone."

"The French are extremely friendly. There is a social aspect to it for them. The communal meals, the wine. But I like it alone."

"I do, too. But I need to go see if they have space for me here."

"Full."

"Are you sure?"

"I just heard them turn a couple away."

I found a receptionist and she confirmed that they were in fact full. I asked if I could pitch my tent somewhere nearby and eat dinner with the other guests.

"Of course, it's no problem. You can put it around the back, or up by the lake. It's very pretty."

"There aren't any other refuges nearby, are there?"

"Not so close. Maybe three hours on the other side of the col."

"The lake it is then."

I rejoined Dave at his table and rummaged around my bag for lunch.

"My wife," Dave said, "she didn't want me to go. She said if I went, she was leaving."

"Really? But you've done this before, right?"

"Last time I told her it was the last time."

"Why doesn't she come with you?"

He gave me a look.

"Right," I said. "It's a tough sell. It's long. It's sort of boring. It's hard. I get it. I couldn't believe Colin came out here at all. Maybe your wife's just worried about you?"

"No, she's just controlling. She wants her way." He checked his phone.

"That her?"

"No, I haven't heard from her since I left. No messages, no emails. Nothing."

It was a sad story, and I was really starting to feel bad for him when Monika popped over the hill, smiled, and walked to our table.

"What are you doing here?" I asked.

"I'm staying here tonight. I said this yesterday."

"I must not have been paying attention. That's great, though. Me too, sort of. They're full, so I'm finally using my tent tonight up by the lake."

Dave was following our back-and-forth politely, pitching little sandwiches of salami and cheese into his mouth one after another. Remarkably, he and Monika had not met, so I introduced them. The route had come to feel like a summer camp to me, a place where I see the same fifteen people at random intervals and never get to know most of them.

Sometime around one in the afternoon, a surprisingly cold wind came up over the mountains and brought opaque clouds down onto us. I started to rethink a night out in bad weather at that altitude and paged through a French guidebook I had picked up in Modane. I couldn't read most of it, but it had very good charts and maps and a list of refuges with phone numbers. I circled one that looked close and asked the recep- tionist if she wouldn't mind calling to see if they had any room available.

"Of course," she said. "It's no problem. I will call."

They did have room and she booked me for half-board—a bed, dinner, and breakfast.

"It' a very nice refuge," she said. "Italian."

My night under the stars dashed, I said good-bye to Mon- ika and Dave once again and, in biting wind, headed for the Col de la Vallée Étroite a few minutes away. It was marked by a wooden cross that floated in the dense fog. For many years, the col was the official border between France and Italy. When the Paris Peace Treaties were signed in 1947, the frontier was redrawn and the col was fully incorporated into France. It now marks the line between the departments—administrative divisions—of Savoie and Hautes-Alpes. All of which is to say that I was now in the third of five departments I would have to walk through to get to Nice.

The Vallée Étroite, or narrow valley, was made all the narrower when I arrived by roving packs of Italians—huge multigenerational families who were determined to enjoy the weather, which was much better at the lower altitude, with a stroll through the valley and back to their cars. Even though we were technically in France, it was more easily accessed by roads from the Italian side. All the signs were in Italian, and French was scarcely heard. I also got the sense, through talking to a few Italians, of a very long and low-simmering dispute over the territory.

"Okay, yes, on a map it is France," one man said to me, "but it is Italy."

Another said that "many, many" Italians had been living in the area before the war, but now there are none. "Still, we come because it is Italian."

I was happy to have this small espresso-strong taste of Italy without actually having to leave France. Land disputes aside, everyone seemed pleased as punch to be there (which may have been because there were so few French present, most of whom apparently choose to pass through rather than stay the night).

The patio in front of my *rifugio* felt distinctly Italian. Surrounded by sheer cliffs and dense woods that crawled up the sides of the valley, people sat sipping coffee, drinking Peroni, and smoking cigarettes. Feeling decadent, I ordered a hot chocolate from the Italian barista. It was a thick soup with the viscosity of wood glue, nothing like the thin stuff I was used to. That's not to say it wasn't delicious, just that I had to eat it with a spoon.

Dinner was phenomenal, a proper feast. What a shame Colin left when he did. He would have enjoyed every bit of it, from the Aperol spritz, the polenta, and the wine (no extra charge) to the warm showers and soft beds. Most of the conversation was conducted in Italian, so I understood even less than usual. The man sitting next to me quietly nodded along for most of the meal, then asked me in English if I spoke Italian.

"Not a word. I'm just getting the hang of French."

"Me neither. I am Belgian. But I love this refuge. I come here every year. You are climbing Thabor?"

"No. I'm walking to Nice."

"Ah, it's a spectacular route. Have you ever walked in Romania?"

"No," I said. "Is there good walking there?"

"The walking is very good, but you must be careful."

"Of Romanians?"

"Of dogs. They do not train their dogs like the French, to bark but not to bite. The Romanian dogs will attack you."

"That sounds terrifying."

"I was walking in Romania last year."

"Did you have problems with dogs?"

"Yes. I was attacked by one dog. Then ten dogs. They were biting me all over. I covered my face, but they bit on my face."

"Jesus," I said.

"Finally, the farmer comes and pulls the dogs away. But I was very badly injured. I had to stay two nights with the farmer, and then I was taken by helicopter to a city hospital."

"That's unbelievable. You could have died."

"Many people die in Romania from dogs. I prefer France."

"I guess I do, too. My family comes from Romania, actually, a long time ago." I had no idea why I said this, even though it is true. The Belgian looked displeased. "But we were run out of the country a long time ago," I added. "Probably by dogs."

At breakfast the next morning, the Belgian introduced me to a Frenchman at the table who spoke less English than perhaps anyone I have ever met. The Belgian then launched into a detailed explanation—in French—of his route, which he had cobbled together himself without the help of any guides. "It is my own creation," he said. It was ludicrously complicated, using sections of a dozen other walking routes in the area to go in a large circle and end up where he started. Then, at the urging of the Frenchman, the Belgian translated a story about the Frenchman getting very lost the year before somewhere in the Pyrenees and spending a freezing night in nothing but a light jacket. "He was cold and alone and fighting vicious birds," said the Belgian.

Anxious to get moving, I finished my coffee and left the two men to swap horror stories of getting attacked by animals. But forty-five minutes later, high on a hill above the valley, the French- man caught up with me. He was sweating profusely, like he'd been going at a full sprint, and wiping his forehead every few seconds with a soaked rag. I moved aside to let him pass, but he apparently wanted to walk together. He must have run out of gas catching up to me, because when we finally started moving, his pace was glacial.

Not only did he not speak English, but he also couldn't understand my French, either. Our conversation, which, astonishingly, lasted hours, consisted entirely of names of towns, cols, mountains, and valleys in the area followed by a *oui* or *non* in reference to the named place (presumably, *"oui"* meant that he had been to the place, or had at least heard of it; I never figured out what *"non"* meant). At a junction on the trail, the signs contradicted the book, and my French friend insisted I follow the sign, but I had trusted my guide up to then and had no reason to doubt it now. Besides, I wasn't about to take advice from a man who just a few hours earlier had admitted to getting lost in the mountains and attacked by birds. I went right. He went left. I never saw him again. (I found out later that either direction would have worked; left crossed the border into Italy and climbed high into the mountains. Right stayed low and was more direct.)

In Plampinet, I took a room at the first auberge I saw. It had two small beds and a sink; the shower was down the hall. So far, I was the only guest. Outside, the sun drenched the village and turned the white stones gold. I sat in the shade under a larch tree and started thumbing through Ian Frazier's book on the Great Plains, a book I'd had on my shelf for years but for whatever reason had never considered reading. I suppose I figured: why read it when I had spent my life living it? Was it a coincidence, then, that I picked it up at that moment? Or was it something else, homesickness maybe, that brought me at that point in my journey to a story of the Midwestern United States—of flatness and big, blue skies; of the curious, kind people who populate the middle part of my country? Whatever it was, Frazier's words rang like little glass bells: "I fear for the Great Plains because many people think they are boring." And this: "In the minds of many, natural beauty means something like Switzerland." The Great Plains are indeed boring, and I would never have called Kansas beautiful, but when I read that line, I missed home terribly. Or I missed my family, the friends I grew up with, my dog, the pleasant blandness of day-to-day life in what might be the blandest, most pleasant place in the world.

17

From Kansas City, you can drive four hundred miles—roughly the distance from Geneva to Nice—west on Interstate 70 and still be forty miles short of the Colorado line. For the first two hundred miles, you hit a city every hour or so: Lawrence, Topeka, Junction City, Salina. The farther you go, the smaller they get. And then civilization tapers off, and there is nothing but tiny towns that most Kansans have never even heard of, towns they don't make letters small enough for on maps. Wilson. Quinter. Brewster. There are Walmarts and McDonalds and rusty filling stations, and then there aren't even Walmarts. When you get to Kanorado, you are 433 miles from the house I grew up in, and you still haven't left the state. Google estimates the drive would take just under six hours, about the same as I was averaging each day in the mountains.

Once, when I was a kid, my family drove all the way to Denver. I don't remember why. It was the only time we ever drove anywhere farther than Chicago. For years, the ride was the standard by which I measured all things boring. It was interminable, hell in a midsized sedan (an Oldsmobile Cutlass probably, maroon). My mom fidgeted in the front seat, and my brother and I teased our little sister because there was nothing else to do. My dad kept his eye on the road. The only high points came when we stopped to stretch our legs and fill up on gas station donuts and bags of gummy bears.

The highway through Kansas curves just enough to keep you awake. When it's too straight, you fall into a trance because nothing outside the car appears to be moving. There are no trees to tell you how fast you are going. No natural landmarks or landscape, just land.

My father is a traveling salesman. He has spent most of his life crossing the Midwest in his car, and as far as I know, he loves it. He does not find it boring or beautiful. But I suspect there is something meditative about the movement. He says it lets him think. He knows the small towns, the blue highways, the rivers, the weather patterns. For four months of each year, he is "on the road." It's impossible to imagine him doing anything else.

As luck would have it, I found myself driving east across the entire state of Kansas exactly one year to the day after I started walking in the mountains. I woke up in a motel in Colby and drove, alone, nearly four hundred miles back to the house I grew up in. In a single day, I covered in a car what took me weeks to walk in France. In an airplane, it would have taken an hour. You can't imagine how fast it feels to drive, or to fly, until you've walked.

It occurs to me, though, that walking in the mountains is a remarkably similar experience to driving on the plains. The scenery moves so slow that you never feel like you are making any progress. A mile might as well be ten miles or a hundred. And then you realize woods have turned to meadows, meadows to mountains, corn fields to wheat. You're over a rocky col and in a town. You're under a tree reading, or in bed, thinking about home.

The book put the walk from Plampinet to the fortified city of Briançon at seventeen miles—almost nine hours—and I didn't see a single soul for the duration. I left Plampinet quietly, as if I had never been there, still feeling homesick, still thinking about the plains. The path twisted up a gravel trail until I could see all the way down the length of the Vallée de la Clarée, which was only just waking up to the early morning light.

I stopped to take a picture of a clump of bright red flowers and made a note to look up what they were. People I met were always talking about the flowers, sharing pictures of them with one another. I never noticed flowers when I was walking; I don't know anything about flowers. But it would be nice to be able to name a few, I thought, when people ask. There is something unnatural about the photograph of the red flowers as I'm looking at it today. The flowers are not growing out of the ground but are set on a tree stump, which is not how I remembered seeing them. They are brighter, too. They look fake. There is no context for them, and I have nothing in my notes, either. I could never caption a photo like this at this point. Maybe for this reason, I like the picture even more. It will always only be a weird picture of red flowers in the woods. I have many memories of the mountains like this, memories I can't fit anywhere in particular, but very few pictures of them.

Ahead and to the right, a wild rocky slope, which I took to be the climb of the day, loomed awfully large. But the closer I got to it, the smaller it looked, which was common, until it revealed a much larger hill behind it. Even though I was in far better shape than when I started, I still dreamt of short days on flat ground. I dreaded climbing, if now only for the painful descent that inevitably followed.

Near a cluster of chalets, I stopped at a fountain to fill up my water bottles, which I'd forgotten to do in Plampinet. I didn't see a *potable* sign, but I didn't see a *nonpotable* sign, either. There was a plaque with a great deal of French on it that I couldn't understand and a diagram of water coming out of a tap. It all looked safe enough. I refilled and moved on.

The trail gained two thousand feet in the next hour and a half, a punishing ascent that early in the day. The Col de Dormillouse, when I reached it, revealed yet another col, hundreds of feet higher. It was at the far end of the light-brown line of the trail. Looking backwards, I could see it unbroken for miles until it was the width of a hair. Farther back sat a row of very high mountains and, behind those, another row, even higher and still covered in snow. Inexplicably, I had crossed both.

Ahead, the path raked to the right like the lightest stroke of an artist's pencil and rose gracefully to the Col de la Lauze above a grassy brown crater below. Near the tops of the peaks, maybe a hundred and fifty feet above, the grass died out and left only white and gray rocks. Below, the earth was rippled and wrinkled like the skin of a shar-pei. I took another picture here of two dead flowers that I don't remember taking. It's even more confounding than the last.

On the col, I found a giant feather (no picture, just a note in my notebook)—an eagle's. The French guide book devotes several pages to the eagles one can see in these mountains, and I took the feather as a sign that, even if I never saw one, there were actually eagles out here. The wildlife had been a major disappointment thus far. Other than the chamois I saw weeks earlier, the only animals that appeared to live out here were marmots, which were so common I didn't even look up anymore when I heard their annoying whistle. The eagle's feather was pointing up toward the ridge to the summit. I could see a faint trail up to the top and briefly considered climbing it because—to paraphrase George Mallory—it was there. Instead, I stepped over the other side of the col and stayed on course.

Montgenèvre, which claims to be one of the first ski resorts in France, was another ghost town, full of shuttered stores and empty ski lifts swinging creepily midslope. I stopped at a large obelisk honoring Napoleon, who, I read in the book, had improved the route through the town and marched his armies over the Col de Montgenèvre (as had Caesar, Charlemagne, and Charles VIII). The monument was inscribed on all four sides: French, Latin, Italian, and Spanish. Behind the monument was a red-and-white big-top circus tent with a flag flapping in the wind. Had there been any people about, it might not have been so depressing. But I was utterly alone, and all of France appeared to have been evacuated overnight.

I gave up the day's walk thirty minutes from Briançon when I stumbled on a rambling gîte in one of the suburbs on the outskirts of the city. It was buried in a neighborhood and run by an energetic woman and her husband. She showed me the bedroom, the dining room, and a perfectly shaded garden in the back where four marvelously healthy retirees were drinking wine and laughing like a living Celebrex commercial.

I sat down and introduced myself to the man across the table. He was called Pierre. Pierre, his wife, his wife's sister, and her husband were on a two-week cycling trip. They did something like this every year, he said. They had no real route, preferring instead to choose a new way each day.

"I am finished with routes," he said.

I laughed. "I am nothing without my route. I am all route."

"You are hiking around Briançon?"

"I am walking to Nice. From Geneva."

His eyes lit up. "La Grande Traversée!" he exclaimed. "*C'est magnifique!*"

"Have you walked it?"

"Yes, once. La Grande Traversée des Alpes. It is an absolutely classic line. A beautiful route. Even on a map it is a work of art, as natural as the mountains themselves. My brother-in-law walked sections of it for five years. All the way from Holland. I walked only from Geneva. But I summited a couple peaks on the way. How old are you?"

"Twenty-nine."

"Good. Many young French don't know the routes. They don't care. But walking in the mountains is French. Like wine or cheese. It's a shame."

"Maybe they don't know about it."

"Everyone my age knows the route. All the routes."

"A lot of people walk the Camino de Santiago in Spain. More people every year, I think."

"Yes. I have done this, too. From France, through the Pyrenees. The Pyrenees are incredible, but that is a pilgrimage and much of it is very boring. I was bored. I was thinking of the Alps the whole time!"

"So why did you do it?"

"I love walking."

"Even when it's hard?"

"When it is hard, you enjoy it more. You feel strong. When it is too easy, it's like walking the dog."

"I do feel strong," I said.

"How long have you been walking?"

"Twenty days, I think."

"And why? Why the mountains? Why the Alps?"

"To walk," I said proudly, as if that were enough.

He smiled. "To walk. Of course. You are strong. For an American," he laughed.

Suddenly, however, I felt very weak, as if all the blood had somehow drained out of my body. I must have looked like people do in films when they realize they've been poisoned—sweaty and panic-stricken—because Pierre asked if I was all right. I excused myself from the table and shuffled grimly through another family's party that was carrying on in the dining room to the bedroom and collapsed on my sleeping bag. Flat on my back, I tried to slow my breathing. I was dripping sweat from my forehead and had a pounding headache. I shut my eyes. Very quickly, my stomach turned over and I jumped to the toilet across the hall and vomited violently. Food poisoning, I guessed. Feeling a little better, I limped back to bed. Hoping I had gotten rid of whatever made me ill, I walked downstairs to ask when dinner would be ready, but as soon as I caught the thick nauseating smell of cooking butter I became sick again.

I spent the next two hours in bed, very still, trying desperately to wish my illness away. By dinner I was a bit better, good enough to join the cyclists at the table.

"You should drink some tea," one of the women said.

"And some mineral water," said another.

"Here," Pierre added, "have some cheese."

186

I looked down at the cheese plate in front of me and realized immediately that this was not a good idea. Apologetically, I excused myself from dinner, ran back upstairs to the toilet, and threw up again. The rest of the night, or as much of it as I remember, followed a similar pattern. Bed, toilet, bed, toilet. Lie down a few minutes, rush to the toilet. I was sharing the room with two other people, climbers, I think. In the middle of the night, I finally propped myself up against the inside of the bathroom door to sleep. I have had long, terrible nights sick from something I ate but none as long or as terrible as that night. My body was on a mission to empty itself, and it did so with absolute fury until my insides were convulsing involuntarily and I was just dry-retching over the toilet, wishing I were dead.

Sometime around four in the morning I fell asleep in the bathroom and didn't wake until eleven the next morning in bed, a reprehensibly late hour at a walker's gîte where most people are up at seven and out the door by eight. I was shaky and weak, but the purging had ceased. I drank some water and sat at the table in the garden. Pierre and his friends were still there, getting ready to leave.

"Feeling better?"

"A little, yeah."

"Something you ate?"

"Maybe. Actually, I think I might have drunk from the wrong fountain yesterday."

"There was no sign?"

"I don't remember."

"You must take care. Rest today."

"I'm only going to Briançon, so I should be ok."

"Good luck, strong man," he said. "And be careful in the south. There are wolves there that come from Italy. Last year a man was killed walking in the mountain."

The wolves would have to wait. My first priority was standing up long enough to pack. Then I had to put my bag on. And then I had to walk thirty minutes to the old fortified center of Briançon, where I would need to find a hotel.

Packing was slow. Lifting my bag was considerably harder since my arms felt like they'd been borrowed from the body of a ten-year-old. I managed to get the bag to a table top and slip myself into the straps. I took a few pathetic steps toward the door and, satisfied that I could actually carry it, walked outside, grabbed my poles, and left. It was not an easy journey. I had to stop and lean against a wall every few minutes to rest, and I sweated uncontrollably even though the sun wasn't up yet and the air was cool. It took over an hour to reach the Porte de Pinerolo, the gate to the city on its north side.

On a narrow cobbled street, I found a row of small hotels and paid for a room at the first one. It was on the third floor, and by this time I was not feeling well at all. I mounted the three flights, which were more difficult than anything I'd climbed outside, and once in the room drank a half-liter of water and fell into the bed. I woke up eighteen hours later to the grating sounds of *Keeping up with the Kardashians* reruns on the TV.

I had planned on resting the day in Briançon and leaving the next morning, but this now struck me as idiotic and probably dangerous. I could barely make it downstairs and up again; a day of walking would kill me. Anyway, I reminded myself, it was not a race. I could stay here a week if I wanted to. Though I would have preferred not to have drunk toxic water, the timing was fortunate. Briançon is not only a relatively large, fully functional city (the last one before I would get to Nice); it is the highest town in France (and the second highest in Europe), over four thousand feet above the sea. In terms of distance, it is roughly halfway between Geneva and Nice, and because of this I had come to think of the first half of the journey as ascent and the second as descent, with Briançon right in the center. The city gave the line a kind of symmetry, as if the south side were a mirror image of the north. Lake Geneva, Briançon, the Mediterranean; water, mountain, water.

Briançon, I learned when I forced myself out of bed and to the tourist office, was not always called Briançon. To the Romans, it was Brigantium and it formed a kind of crossroads on the way west and south. But the city really came into its own in the seventeenth century, when King Louis XIV's chief military engineer Sébastien Le Prestre de Vauban designed and built a series of fortifications aimed at keeping just about everyone out. For forty years, Vauban was very busy fortifying cities along France's borders, and Briançon is one of several hundred places where his work is on display.

As a result of Vauban's engineering, the city feels like a cross between every other small French town I'd been in and a large prison. High walls run around the perimeter and inside, and a dizzying tangle of stairs run up and down to other fortified buildings on several hills. It was like wandering around inside an M.C. Escher drawing. If the purpose was to disorient, it was wildly successful. I was laughably lost within minutes, trying to figure out if I was in the same spot as before or if it just looked the same. On the east side of the city, I took a set of stone ramps to a fort high above the city. Near the top I was so dizzy I had to lie down on the cool stone until I was reasonably sure I wouldn't throw up. From the fort, I could see the entire city below, squeezed into Vauban's walls. Above, the city looked even more confusing. The cathedral's two towers—one with a sundial, one with a clock—marked the northwest side of the city. (I made a note to get a closer look when I walked back down but, of course, forgot when I got to the bottom.) Beyond that, the plan of the city was utterly indecipherable.

It was late afternoon, and the Grande Rue was bustling with tourists. I walked past a shop selling souvenirs, a book store, a bank. A girl made crêpes at a stand across from a fountain where a team of cyclists was filling up their bottles. Families stopped to order crêpes. An older couple walked by, smiling and holding hands. A busy city can be the loneliest place in the world, far lonelier than up in the mountains. In the mountains, solitude feels perfectly natural.

I walked down to a parking lot that overlooked the Jardin du Gouverneur. In the shade of a tree that had grown up through the asphalt, I noticed out of the corner of my eye the small red-and-white route marker painted onto the tree. It seemed a very sudden reminder of what I was doing there, how far I had come, and how much farther I had to go. I reached out to touch it as if it might disappear and I might wake up from a strange dream, a dream in which I thought it was a good idea to try to walk across the Alps. Then I turned around and limped weakly back to the hotel.

"Jon?" I knew the voice, but I had to look up from my book to make sure it was real.

"Monika!" I said, thrilled once again to see a familiar face. "What are you doing here?"

"I am finished," she said. "Today was my last day walking. I am going back to Zurich tomorrow morning."

"That's right. I forgot you were ending in Briançon. Congratulations. How does it feel?"

"Very strange. It's like this every time. You can't imagine going back to the regular world."

We caught up on the last few days. She said it was a good idea I hadn't stayed in my tent at the refuge near Thabor. The weather had only gotten worse. And a woman she spoke to who had camped by the lake said it was one of the most miserable nights of her life—terribly cold and wet with a roaring wind that kept trying to rip the tent from the ground and send it flying off the mountain.

"We had free wine at my Italian refuge," I said. "And the food was amazing. They served Aperol spritzes before dinner."

"It seems I made a mistake, too, then. I should have come with you."

"Next time," I said. "Find the Italian huts."

"Yes. Next time."

"Will you come back to finish?" I asked. "Briançon to Nice is supposed to be beautiful. People keep telling me it's 'wild,' whatever that means."

"I don't know. Physically, it is okay for me. But emotionally, I find it hard. It is hard to begin, and then it becomes hard to leave. I can't believe on Monday I will be in my office, thinking only of work."

I laughed. "By next summer, you will be thinking of the mountains. I have no doubt."

"You are probably right. So you will leave tomorrow?"

"I hope so. If I'm feeling right. I wanted to leave today but it was impossible. I could barely walk around Briançon. And I still have no appetite. I'm just drinking mineral water by the liter and trying to stay upright."

"Please rest. And drink only the safe water from now on."

"Lesson learned," I said. "How is your hotel?"

"I'm staying here."

"At this hotel?"

"Yes. And so is Dave. Have you seen him?"

"He's here, too?"

"Yes."

The three of us ate dinner at the hotel. We toasted Monika, said our farewells, and grew sappy about the mountains as the night went on. Dave would be leaving the next day, as well, he said, but going twice as far as I and not resting again until he got to Nice. We agreed to meet there if I arrived within a day of him. With both of them gone, I thought, it would be like starting from scratch. I wouldn't know anyone anymore. The faces at dinner the next evening would be entirely unfamiliar. We all agreed to stay in touch and I promised Monika I would let her know when I was finished. But how many times have I agreed to stay in touch with someone, only to never contact them again? How many promises had I made, in how many countries, and then broken—out of laziness or apathy or indifference or for a hundred other reasons—without a second thought? Too many to count.

Part Three
Walking

18

I woke up early to a sound I almost didn't recognize: the dampened *tap-tap-tap* of rain falling on pavement. Immediately, I was back in Geneva, unable to sleep in my air-conditioned hotel room, the rain drumming on the window. I looked outside and saw it was just a drizzle, the soft showers that fall in the morning. It was seven, but I couldn't get out of bed. I fell asleep again and woke an hour later. Still raining. I checked my phone and found an email. It was from Bernard, whom I hadn't seen in weeks. I had forgotten that we'd even exchanged email addresses. He and Michel were still walking together and were three days from Nice, he wrote. How was I doing? Had I made it to Briançon yet? He had a hotel recommendation for me (the hotel I and everyone else was staying at, apparently the only hotel in Briançon). "I'm very proud of you to be still on your way."

When I left the hotel, I was somewhere else. I felt the rain, but it didn't bother me. After a few minutes, I barely noticed it. My legs moved, but out of habit more than anything else. I did not consult the map or the book. I didn't need to. I saw the route markers—signs—everywhere I looked. I followed them, robotically, down a set of winding ramps to the Porte d'Ebrun on the west side of the city. Barely outside of the high old city, on the far side of the gate directly over the passageway, was an inscription: "*Le passé répond de l'avenir.*" I jotted it down in my notebook.

Southwest of the fortified city, Briançon spread out in end-less suburbs. I'm sure I got lost. Eventually I reached the train station, which I knew was on my route, and from there decided to follow the book as closely as I could: "Walk up the road, but watch for a path climbing left, between a small field and a large building. Continue up a road to reach a village and a prominent church tower." But there were small fields and large buildings and villages and church towers everywhere. I wondered if I was overexerting myself, if I should turn back and spend another night in Briançon—a few more nights, a week, maybe. Or just end things here. I'd walked some two hundred miles, which is something to be proud of. It's a lot of walking. It's enough, if there's such a thing. What more would I get out of another one hundred or two hundred miles? More pain? More weather? But I knew I wouldn't stop. It was a fantasy I let myself get carried away with to take my mind off walking.

Near the top of a village—the one from the book—before the path went into the forest, I was joined unwittingly by a small black dog. Like a guide I didn't know I needed, she ran up ahead of me and waited until I caught up, then ran ahead again. Sometimes she got distracted by something in the trees and jumped into the woods to investigate. But she always came back out and waited for me. The dog did this long enough that I started to worry she wouldn't find her way home. The deeper into the woods we moved, the closer to me she stayed until we were walking alongside each other. When I passed a British couple, I asked if she was theirs. They had thought she was mine, they said. When we walked out of the forest a couple of hours later, the dog abruptly turned around and disappeared back into the trees.

The climb to the Col des Ayes, which marks the entrance to the Parc Naturel Régional du Queyras, one of France's many designated nature preserves, was long and slow. I knew my heart wasn't in it that day. Whether I was still sick or I'd simply had enough of the whole thing, I didn't know. But it was a slog, boring and wet, then boring and hot. I had read somewhere, and made a note in my notebook, that Air France pilots call the Queryas the "blue hole" because of its consistently clear skies. In good weather, you can see back to Briançon and on to Mount Viso. When I stepped up on the col, of course, rain clouds were forming to the south, and it felt like a certainty that I would walk through a storm before the day ended. At the moment, however, the sun was bearing down on me, heating the wet ground enough to cause steam to rise out of it.

I looked down over a meadow fifteen hundred feet below with a small chalet and an emerald green lake. If I weren't on a tight schedule, especially with the clouds, I would have liked to stop at the chalet, knock on the door, and meet the people who lived there. There is never enough time to see everything you want to see, to talk to people, to explore. Even in wild places, you find yourself stuck on some kind of schedule. You have to be here by this time, there by that time; you need food, sleep. I passed on without so much as stopping and walked the gravelly road until it opened onto a parking lot and rolled into a forest. Through a break in the trees, I saw a large patch of green grass a few miles ahead that I hoped was Brunissard. I'd been walking in a sour mood all day, and all I wanted to do was crawl into a bed and fall asleep.

Even the forest was depressing. All the trees had been ripped from the ground or twisted unnaturally so that they stabbed straight out horizontally. The ground was covered with large rocks. I guessed it was the result of a landslide, but it looked more like the footage we used to see after a tornado tears some small town apart in southern Kansas. I climbed over downed trunks that were still soggy from rain. It was odd to see such devastation contained to such a small area. It couldn't have been more than a mile until everything was right again, the trees green and strong, with little drops of water hanging off the needles and shining like Christmas lights.

It began to rain when I reached Brunissard. Most of the last stretch had been on hard pavement, and my feet were killing me. My soles had softened over the last few days. Either that, or they were just breaking down.

I was told, rather coldly, by the manager of the only lodgings I could find that there was no room for me and that I should have made a reservation. There were campgrounds a couple miles back, she said. I had made a mental note of the campgrounds on my way in, as a last resort, but was really hoping for a soft bed and hot food. I checked the book. Thirty minutes on was a small village, La Chalp, that had a gîte. But if it was full, it would be even farther from the campgrounds, and I would have to double back several miles in the rain. Or I could keep moving and sleep somewhere in the mountains.

The path to La Chalp is just a main road. There is nothing sadder than walking down the side of a road in the rain. Even now—especially now—the sight of some sad sack walking on the side of the road when it is pouring breaks my heart. Between the weather, the pain in my feet (my knees, too), the rude hotel manager, the uncertainty of the next town, and the rest of the goddamn walk, I felt like an asshole. An idiot. I wanted to be dry, and warm, and done. Maybe there's a bus from La Chalp, I thought. Or I could hitch a ride to Nice. I could be there in half a day. The southern Alps are hotter, dryer, and emptier than the high mountains in the north. The stages are longer, water and food fewer and farther between. If I moved quickly, I figured it would take ten more days of hard walking. But these were things I tried not to think about.

There were, in fact, several places to sleep in La Chalp. That was almost all there was, actually. The gîte was empty, but it was warm and it felt like a home, with a comfortable dining room, a real bathroom and shower, and a few small bedrooms.

"You are the only guest tonight, so far," the young woman who ran the place said. Her name was Sophie.

"Would you close if there were no guests?" I asked.

"Of course not. You never know when someone will come in. Sometimes at midnight."

"Either way," I said, "I'm grateful. It's been a miserable day walking."

"Relax. I will make dinner."

In a soft chair by a snapping fire in the living room, I read, over and over, a line on the final page of Frazier's Plains book:

Now, when I have trouble getting to sleep, I sometimes imagine that my bed is on the back of a flatbed pickup truck driving across the Great Plains.

Something about it—the image, maybe, or the rhythm of the words—struck me that night, in that moment, as impossibly beautiful. I closed my eyes and pictured myself lying on a bed in the back of a truck, somewhere in Kansas. I have no idea where it's going, but it doesn't matter because it's all basically the same. The road is flat at first until, after a while, I can feel the gentle roll of hills. I'm looking at the stars, which I realize I haven't seen once in the mountains. Dawn breaks, and the sky turns a fiery orange. The truck stops abruptly and I sit up. In front of me is the ocean, gorgeous and glass-smooth. I get out of the truck and walk toward the water. Soft, sun-warmed sand fills the spaces between my toes. I'm only a few steps away. I count them: one, two, three, four. Something wet falls on my skin and I look up. Rain. A little at first, and then tons of it, tearing the ocean to shreds before I can reach it.

I woke up when the door slammed shut and saw two men covered from head to toe in shiny, black rain suits.

"*Bonjour*," one said across the room.

"*Bonjour*."

"Sorry to wake you."

"It's no problem," I said getting up. "You were out walking in this?"

"Yes. Damn rain. Miserable fucking rain." They were both busy unzipping and unstrapping their layers of rain gear and hanging them on the patio to dry.

"I'm Vincent, and this is my friend Bruno."

"Jon."

"Jon. Where are you from?"

"The US."

"California?"

I laughed. "Kansas, actually"

"Wow. It's very flat in Kansas. The wild west."

"You can't imagine how flat it is." I said. "You're French?"

"Swiss."

They were from Lausanne and were walking from Briançon to Menton, a town on the sea next to the Italian border. It was their first day.

"Damn hard today," Vincent said.

"Fahking hard." Bruno added. Bruno's English was not as good as his friend's, but he had the basics down.

"The Queyras," Sophie interjected, "was for a long time a refuge for French protestants. It is very remote. Very difficult to access. Still today there are many protestants in the Queyras."

"It feels very far away from everything," I said, "but I can't tell if that's just me."

We dug into a feast of homemade soup, *paupiettes de veau*, and pasta and my mood brightened with the first spoonful for the first time all day.

Sophie went on: "It has some of the highest villages in France and is protected by mountains on all sides. It is a very safe place."

(I grew even happier with the thought that I was in a safe place with good, hot food and surrounded, once again, by such friendly people.)

"And tomorrow is St. Bartholomew's Day."

"What is St. Bartholomew's Day?"

"The day the Catholics killed many protestants in France. In Paris and all over the country."

"God," I said. "Recently?"

"Maybe four hundred and fifty years ago." She served the *fromage blanc* with fig jam.

The massacre had started that night, actually, on the twenty-third of August, 1572, when King Charles IX ordered the deaths of several Huguenot leaders. The killing spread and lasted weeks until, as Sophie put it, "many, many thousands were dead."

I left La Chalp just as I had arrived: cold, tired, and pissed on by rain. And alone—the Swiss were not even awake when I left. Though I'd slept well, free from nightmares of Catholic mobs chasing Protestants into the hills and murdering them, my body was not cooperating. A few days earlier, I had felt like I was getting stronger, growing more attuned to the mountains. But now it felt like I'd turned a corner and was simply falling apart, piece by piece: feet first, then knees, shoulders, and legs.

The rain let up after an hour, and I managed to dry off a little walking up through some woods to Fort Queyras, an imposing jumble of fortifications built on a hill high in the mountains. It dates back to the middle of the thirteenth century and was further fortified by Vauban in the seventeenth. From underneath, it looked a lot like Briançon, and I'm ashamed to admit that on that day, I couldn't be bothered to go inside. I walked straight past it, first to a small gift shop selling post cards and candy (I bought candy), and then through the town. I must have been a walking zombie because I found out later that I'd strolled right past a museum dedicated to the formation of the Alps housed in a crypt, something I would not have missed if my head had been on right.

I came to a large meadow on relatively flat land with a small wooden cabin on raised slats. I wondered if I could just hide out in the cabin and wait. But wait for what? For better weather? For a ride out of the mountains? A deafening thunderclap broke me out of my thoughts. But the sky was clear, and the echo made it hard to tell where the sound was coming from, if a storm had already passed or was on the way. Another clap, to the west. I stopped walking. My legs wouldn't move. I couldn't have walked if I'd wanted to, much less through a storm at eight thousand feet. Not on that day, and not alone. I was still two hours from the col and at least three from Ceillac, the nearest town with shelter. Fuck it, I thought. Fuck this whole stupid walk and this shitty weather and the magic of the Alps and everything else. While I was standing there, clouds rolled in like an invading army and went to work dumping rain all over me.

I walked ten minutes back to the cabin, jumped the fence, and climbed a set of stairs to a small deck. The doors and windows were shuttered, but I knocked anyway. If someone was there, I figured I would ask if I could stay the night or at least until the storm passed. No one answered, so I took a seat on a chair under the awning and tried to collect myself. It was still early enough in the day that I could waste a few hours sitting here and still get to Ceillac in time for dinner, though I would be cutting it very close. And I had no reservation, so there might not be room anyway.

After forty-five minutes, the rain showed no sign of giving up. Through the deluge, I saw the shape of a man walking the path toward me. He was alone and looked miserable.

"*Bonjour*," I shouted.

He looked up at me and shouted back. "Jon?"

"Vincent?"

"Have you seen Bruno?"

"No. You're the first person I've seen since the fort."

"Damn. I don't know where he is. I thought he was ahead of me."

He joined me under the awning and pulled out his phone.

"Your phone works out here?"

"Sometimes. But he is not answering. Damn bad weather. I'll wait for him here, it's okay?"

"Be my guest. I was going to wait for the storm to pass."

"It's a massive storm. I saw on my weather this morning."

"That's why I don't look at the weather anymore."

We watched the rain, squinting to see Bruno if he happened to pass by. Thirty minutes passed. Forty-five. Every few minutes, Vincent would shout his friend's name and we'd listen for a response. Finally, we heard something.

"Vincent!"

"Bruno!

"Vincent!"

"Bruno!"

He came out of the rain and under the cabin, looking terrible but relieved. He had been ahead of Vincent but had taken a wrong turn at some point and gotten "a little lost." With the rain hammering down around us, we ate lunch and decided to keep moving. After all, what other option did we have?

"If we move quickly," Vincent said, "it's maybe one hour to the col and one hour to the town. Two hours in the rain."

And move quickly we did. From the cabin to the col, we just about jogged. With each burst of thunder or flash of lightning, we picked up the pace a little more. The Col Fromage lies at 7,500 feet, an altitude far higher than I ever want to be in bad weather. Which is why it felt like a small miracle when, just as we arrived, the rain stopped. A brilliant blue sky teased through the clouds, and a warm wind blew over the mountains. Exhilarated,

Vincent and Bruno high-fived and took pictures of each other. I sat on a rock and caught my breath. I looked up at the clouds, broken and random and shattered, spent, as if they'd worn themselves out throwing weather down on the mountains.

19

The rain started again when we were halfway down on the other side of the col, and it didn't stop until much later that night. Every five minutes, lightning struck close enough to make us jump out of our skin.

The gîte in Ceillac had one bed left and the man I spoke to begrudgingly went back into the kitchen to make sure there was enough food to feed me. Due in large part to the fact that, other than myself, Vincent, Bruno, and a Dutch woman in her thirties, no one inside appeared to be under the age of sixty-five, the place felt more like an old folks' home than a rest stop for hikers. The dining room, with its linoleum tile floors and fluorescent lights, would not have been out of place in a public high school or a hospital.

Waiting for dinner, I spoke to Mary, a woman I'd met briefly when I was lost outside of Briançon. She was sixty-nine, no more than five feet tall, with short red hair and intense, energetic eyes. She was walking with three friends from Briançon to Nice. The oldest among them was seventy-two, the youngest was sixty-four. They were using a sherpa service to ferry their bags from one inn to the next, but they did all the walking on their own. I told her I was still in my twenties (barely) and it was killing me to walk this hard. She laughed.

"Did you walk in the rain?" I asked.

"Of course. It was terrible."

"Isn't it dangerous?"

"It is no more dangerous for me than for you. But yes, it is dangerous. Lightning strikes are very common in such weather. We must be careful."

I sat at the children's table for dinner with Vincent, Bruno, the Dutch girl, and Thomas, a Frenchman from Lorraine who, at sixty, just barely made the cutoff. When everyone retired to bed around eight p.m., I followed suit and spent an awful night sleeping in a damp bag above a man who snored like a strangled hog.

"Today is a day of lakes and wonders," Mary said to me over coffee the next morning.

"And the weather?"

"Perfect. No rain today."

"If I don't see another drop of rain until I get to Nice, I'll be very happy."

"These Alps are much drier than where you came from. But very hot, too. You must drink a lot of water." There was something comforting about a seventy-year-old woman making sure I got plenty of water. Suddenly, I wanted very badly to walk with her group all day, or all the way to Nice, if they'd have me. When I mentioned this, she laughed and said her girls were too slow for me.

"Fine," I said, "But I bet you pass me at some point today."

But first I needed an ATM. I was running low on cash, and based on the guide and the map I couldn't count on finding one in too many places between that town and Nice. I walked back to the center of the town and asked a shop owner if he knew where a cash machine was. He said there wasn't one in town, but that the next town over might have one. I thanked him and walked on until I found someone else who told me she thought there was a machine in the post office, in the center of town. I found the post office around the corner from the first shop owner I had spoken to, but it was closed. It didn't open for a couple of hours. I walked around the building a few times to make sure I wasn't missing it. Why would they put an ATM in a building that's closed most of the time? I walked up to the front door to peek inside and see if anyone was there. I could see the ATM. It was glowing. When I leaned on the door, I felt it give slightly. When I tried pushing it, it moved again. I pulled it and it opened easily, since it had not been locked in the first place.

With enough cash in my wallet to last me until Nice, I left Ceillac behind. I told myself that I felt good, that nothing could stop me. Not rain, not cold, not heat, and not illness. Not even boredom. As long as I kept my feet on the path, I would arrive at my destination. The line is unbroken; if I don't deviate from it, it will carry me to the sea. These are the motivational thoughts one has when one is working to climb a very steep hill early in the morning. They are the kind of thoughts that are powerful in the moment and meaningless later on. But there is a mental aspect to so much walking. Covering long distances, you can't help but spend time in your own head. Rousseau wrote that he could only meditate when he was walking. "When I stop, I cease to think; my mind only works with my legs." Most of the time,

I tried to empty my mind completely, to not think of anything at all. I counted my steps or I tried to list all the places I'd slept since Geneva, a memory game. Or I would make detailed mental notes of the landscape, the shape of leaves, the length of grass, the number of peaks in the distance, the carpet of roots on the forest floor. But such thoughts are a house of cards. The more you stack on top of one another, the quicker they come crashing down. No details can be retained by these mental exercises; they just kill time and keep me from thinking about how much pain I am in, or how hard the climbing is, or how out of breath I am, or how many miles I have left to walk that day, that week, or until I can stop. They keep me from thinking, too, about the many ways I can still hurt myself: a twisted ankle, a bad fall, dehydration, another bout of water poisoning. The trick is to occupy your mind and let your legs do the work.

Two hours from Ceillac, I came to the first lake, Lac Miroir. It was perfectly still. A crowd of walkers were ringing its edge, staring at the upside-down image of the mountains and trying to take pictures of it. I found Thomas, the Lorrainer from dinner the night before, asleep under a tree with his hat over his face. He had applied a layer of sunscreen to his arms and legs that was still white and thick. I found a spot under the shade of another tree and watched people hop around with their cameras.

From Lac Miroir, I climbed a rocky ski piste under an increasingly hot sun. In every photo I have of this climb, the flares from the sun look like sharp daggers stabbing at the dry earth. Which is not unlike how it was starting to feel. The tree I had rested under near the lake turned out to be the last bit of available shade for many miles that day. For the rest of the afternoon, my silly-looking sun hat was the only shield I had against the high altitude heat of the sun. My steps turned laborious, my legs heavy. I wiped sweat from my brow constantly and poured small amounts of water on my head to try to keep cool. A family passed me, all of its members apparently unaffected by the heat, and I wondered what gene they had that I didn't. Though I've always lived in places with miserably hot summers, I've never gotten used to the heat. I've spent many perfectly comfortable spring days worrying about how terrible the coming summer is going to be.

I shuffled up the path to a final climb that led to the second lake, Lac Ste. Anne, a piercing turquoise pool almost eight thousand feet above sea level with a large wooden cross and a small chapel nearby. It was here that I finally caught up with Mary and her slow friends. Vincent and Bruno were there, too. Thomas made it a few minutes later. The sun was scorching, but a breeze blew off the peaks and cooled the area around the lake. Dozens of day hikers from Ceillac made it impossible to take a picture of the scene that didn't include the back of someone's head or a group of smiling people posing with their arms locked around one another's necks. A woman asked if I wanted her to take a picture of me. I declined but then changed my mind. "For my mother," I said. She laughed, took the picture quickly, and handed the phone back to me. I looked at it, astonished. There I was, looking nothing like myself—thinner, tanned, dressed in a hiking costume, and squinting into the sun with the lake behind me. No one else was in the frame. It's one of only a few pictures I have of myself in the Alps.

The Col Girardin, which marks the beginning of Alpes de Haute-Provence, was an hour away and a thousand feet higher. The path stuck to what the book calls "slopes of lustrous, friable, scree." Ten thousand feet above the sea, it's hard to imagine a phrase more frightening than "friable scree," so I tried not to think about it, which only made it harder to ignore. Planting my feet as solidly as possible on the way up, I reached the col, but only after a long, painful crawl.

As always, though, it was the descent that was the problem. This one plummeted straight down on more loose scree for hundreds of feet. An elderly man with no walking sticks passed me on the col as I was getting ready to take the first step and ran down the mountain. I watched him anxiously. My legs shook wildly. I stuck my walking sticks in the ground in the hopes that they would catch me if I slipped. The rocks slid out from under me and made an awful sound, like ripping paper or screeching brakes. I had been on worse descents, but this one affected me more. When I finally did reach a section that leveled out, I looked up and felt like I could collapse. Behind me, a group of people were struggling even more. Three of them were trying to convince a fourth to take a particularly sketchy step across a section of the path that narrowed to only a few inches. On the left side was a badly sloped wall, and on the right nothing, just a sheer drop. The man refused to take the step and a line had formed behind him. It was impossible to go around, so they had no choice but to wait. Still, the man couldn't do it. I felt for him. I had hesitated at the same spot and, knowing the longer I waited the harder it would get, had made the step—but it was a tremendous effort, and terrifying. A few people next to me were watching to see what happened. Finally, the man leaned over, grabbed a friend with his arms, and made the step. It was awful to watch, clumsy and dangerous. You could feel the relief when it was over.

"I saw you up on the col," I said to the man later at the gîte. Hours later his face still showed signs of panic, like someone who had seen a ghost. He drank his beer quickly.

"*Vertige,*" he said. "I could not move. Have you experienced this?"

"I hadn't thought of it like that, but yes, higher up on the col. I could barely get my leg to take the first step down. I couldn't stop shaking. It's strange, actually, now that I think about it. I don't remember worrying so often about the heights until recently."

"Today was our first day in the mountains. We're from the city. I thought I was going to die, seriously. And then I watched someone else take the same step as if it was just a normal step."

"From where I was watching, it looked very dangerous. You could have fallen, for sure. And I remember the place myself, thinking how narrow the path was."

"I was trying only to think of taking the one step. If I can make the step, I can make it to Maljasset, drink my beer, sleep, and go home tomorrow."

"So just one day and you're finished?"

"My friends—colleagues, actually—would like to keep walking. But I don't think I can do it. I don't feel any excitement from today. Only that it is stupid for me to be here. To be honest, I don't understand this obsession many French people have with walking in the mountains. Sometimes they walk for weeks, every day. It's too much."

I laughed. "I've been walking for over three weeks. Not every day, but almost. From Geneva."

"Why?"

"Good question," I said laughing. "A few days ago, near Briançon, someone asked me that and I felt like I knew the answer. Like I had come close to understanding it myself. And then the moment passed. Now it seems like the longer I walk, the harder it is to say what I'm doing here. Sometimes it's really special—the walking, the mountains, the people—and sometimes it's terrible."

He shook his head. "It's madness."

After dinner I tried to read, but I couldn't concentrate. I put on a sweatshirt and went out into the cold evening air. Even in late August, temperatures high up in the mountains tend to stay low during the night. Maljasset is perhaps ten-buildings-large, and at least two of them exist to serve hikers or skiers. At the far eastern edge is a small church dedicated to Saint Antoine. I read on a plaque nailed to the stone that the church was likely built in the thirteenth century. On February 14, 1531, an avalanche destroyed the upper parts of the church. There was also its name: église Saint-Antoine du Désert. I couldn't figure out what was meant by *désert*. I typed the word into a French-English dictionary app on my phone. In the dimming ultramarine light of the world around me, the screen on my phone glowed a ghostly white: Arid; Dry; Barren, it said. Desiccated. Desolate. Lonely.

20

"To Larche?" Thomas asked me, handing me a cup of cold coffee.

"Yes."

"Let's go?"

"*Ensemble?*"

"*Oui.*"

"Sure," I said. "It's a long walk."

"*Oui, vingt-cinq kilomètres.*"

"Twenty-five? I guess that's right. I still think in miles."

"Twenty miles?"

"Something like that, yeah.

It was eight a.m. and the staff was still asleep. Five or six guests were wandering around the dining room waiting for breakfast like cranky children. One of the guys running the place finally came through the door, glassy-eyed and yawning. I drank my cold coffee and studied my guidebook. Seventeen miles to

Larche, with over three thousand feet of climbing and almost five thousand knee-breaking feet of descent. The forecast promised lots of sunshine, which, without the lush woods of the northern Alps, was becoming a mixed blessing. Thomas and I left on the main road. We had only made it half a mile before a car pulled up alongside. It was the late-sleeper from the gîte. He asked if we wanted a ride to the bridge. "The walk is very boring until then and it would save you an hour of walking," he said. On the way, he outlined a route from the bridge that he said was much better than the one we were taking, but harder to find. I couldn't figure out what was better about it, only that we would probably get lost if we tried to take it. Once he let us out of the car, I suggested we stick to the normal route.

The climbing that morning was hard, through thick woods, and Thomas moved slowly. I liked his pace, though. It was measured and steady, calibrated to prevent a burnout. It's how I wish I knew how to walk. It was good to walk with someone, too, even if communication between us was difficult. But he didn't seem to mind the silence and humored me when I tried to speak French.

"*Pin,*" he said, stopping under a large tree.

"Pah?"

"*L'arbre.*"

"The tree?"

He pulled a branch down and held the end up between us. "*Pin.*"

"Oh, pine trees."

"My employment is the forest department."

"You work for the forest department?"

"*Oui.* But I do not know trees. Only *pin* and some others."

"You see those trees over there?" A patch of the woods below us was brown, bruised like an otherwise ripe piece of fruit. "Why are they brown?"

"I don't know," he said. "Perhaps a malady."

The town of Fouillouse was even smaller than Maljasset, and a few minutes beyond the last small structure, all traces of town life disappeared. The landscape changed so drastically and so quickly it felt like we'd walked into another world. The grass was yellow and dry, except for some small wet patches. In the distance, hundreds of sheep grazed on the hills. But for the most part, the land was barren and rocky—desolate. Wind knocked around the high craggy peaks and whistled ominously at us from every direction.

By the first col, the sun was unbearable. I stopped for a few minutes under the shade of a large boulder and pressed my face against the cool stone. I could see the path ahead of me from where I was standing, across a rocky wasteland to the skeletal remains of a military fort. From there, it climbed a grassless slope to another to a col with more abandoned forts. Beyond the col there was a long and steep descent. That was the pattern, and it was true not only of today but of every day I had spent walking, and every day to come. It was a depressing thought in that moment. A small airplane appeared over the mountains and drew circles above me, dipping and climbing like an eagle. It was silent. I listened for the sound of an engine, some mechanical hum. I watched it, thinking that maybe it was a bird. The sun was in my eyes. I pulled my hat down and craned my neck higher.

"A glider," Thomas said.

"There's no sound."

"No engine."

The Baraquements de Viraysse, the barracks belonging to the fort, were roofless and scattered with tufts of old barbed wire. Built in the late 1880s, the fort was one of the highest in the Alps. It had a direct view of Italy and had become a part of the

Alpine line of fortifications on the French-Italian border. It didn't look like it had been used since the forties, and it made an already creepy section of the route that much creepier. Higher up, adjacent to the Col de Mallemort, the rest of the fort looked down on the barracks to one side and Italy on the other. It was a land of ghosts, abandoned buildings, remnants. It was gorgeous in a sad way, like the rotting old mansions I used to see in New Orleans or the slowly fading grandeur of the Hotel Moskva in Belgrade, where I can sit in the café and imagine how splendid the city was at the turn of the century—where I'm sitting now, in fact, thinking about the mountains.

I could have followed a short detour to the fort itself, but it was gloomy enough already. I waited for Thomas on the col and we ate lunch in the narrow shade of a sign post. The sign pointed to where the path picked up the descent. Once again, the drop was sheer and the path a mess of slippery gravel. Thomas bounded down without noticing how terrifying it all was, but I took my usual baby steps. What I would have preferred to do was crawl on all fours. I let an older man pass me and he winked as he did. I tried to watch his footsteps and suss out some technique, but it just looked like his feet would never slip no matter how hard they fell or how loose the ground was under him.

The descent took dozens of switchbacks that only revealed how steep they were once you made the turns. From above, it was impossible to see their true angles. In this way, every few feet came with a new, even more frightening, view of the next few feet. Sometimes, Thomas would wait for me to make sure I didn't fall, and then run ahead. My hands and legs shook uncontrollably. If it hadn't been ninety degrees outside, I would have looked like I was shivering. The only support I had to steady myself were my poles, which I relied on far too heavily.

"*Ça va?*" Thomas asked when I reached the bottom.

"*Ça va*," I lied.

The Ubaye valley spread out before us. Though we could see the town, its World War I memorial slightly higher than the two dozen buildings around it, we were still an hour and a half away. I took a long drink of water before continuing down the mountain. The rocky path from the col turned into a slightly less vertigo-inducing descent on long and level switchbacks. The path had been worked into the side of a grassy hill that still had clumps of wildflowers and lavender growing out of it. My shaking was under control, and I was feeling good about having made it down the col alive, though less good about having to descend a dozen more high, dry cols before I reached Nice. I tried to keep up with Thomas, who was taking giant, confident steps, but couldn't bring myself to walk very quickly, even on flatter ground.

With Larche now only a stone's throw away, and Thomas a hundred feet in front of me, I stepped a bit too heavily on my right foot, which slipped out ahead of me like it was on ice. Instinctively, I stabbed my right pole into the ground, but the shift in weight caused by the slip was too much. My pack threw all of my weight onto my left foot, flipped me over sideways, and then onto my right foot without enough time to plant myself. All of a sudden, I was dashing uncontrollably downhill in long galloping strides, trying to stay upright. At the edge of the hill was a clear fifty-foot drop where a river had cut a deep ravine into the land. I gained more and more speed, my backpack relentlessly pushing me forward. No longer holding onto my poles, my arms flailed wildly and I yelled to Thomas, who turned around and, like a football player, crouched in a position to stop me. I ran into him at full speed, knocked us both down, and took a long time to register the earth beneath me.

Thomas jumped up and dusted himself off. I stayed flat on my back with my eyes closed.

"*Ça va?*"

"I don't know."

"Pain?"

"Not yet, but I'm afraid to move."

"Your legs?"

I propped myself up on my elbows, then rolled over and pushed up on my hands until I was standing. Bending my knees, I braced for piercing jolts of pain, but none came. It was like slicing your hand with a sharp knife and waiting for the blood to come, only it never did.

"I think I'm fine."

"Good. You were fast!"

"Thomas," I said leaning over to put my hands on my knees. "I think you saved my life. I would have gone flying off that cliff if you hadn't been there."

"It's possible," he said.

"I can't believe I'm not hurt. Maybe it's just adrenaline. Am I bleeding?"

"I don't see anything."

"Are you okay?"

"Fine."

"I slipped. My foot slipped and my bag threw me down the mountain."

"This path is not so good. The stones move. You must be careful. I think your body is tired from too much walking."

I walked in circles with my hands on my hips stretching my back and bending my knees. The right knee was sore, but otherwise I was fine.

"Let's get to town." I said. "I've had enough of the mountains today."

We walked the rest of the way to Larche slowly. My mind was empty, blank. I tried to reconstruct the slip, the downhill tear, the crash in my head—but I never got far enough to see how it all happened. The only image I could see with any clarity was one of myself running off the cliff. Had the circumstances been different—if Thomas hadn't been there, or if he'd been behind me, or if we had never even met and I was walking to Larche alone or with Mary and her friends . . .

I sleepwalked into Larche, paid no attention to its war memorial, about which the book had written something that I couldn't remember, and found the gîte on the edge of the city. It was an old-fashioned place, like a youth hostel from the 1970s or a YMCA—basic bathrooms downstairs, a couple of small bedrooms crammed with bunks, and a large dining room. Inexplicably, it was decorated with Tibetan prayer flags and pictures of the Himalayas. I found the manager, a small woman in her sixties or seventies, in the kitchen making dinner.

"*Bonjour*," I said.

She wiped her hands on a dish towel and looked at me.

"Do you have a bed for tonight?" I asked.

"We are almost empty tonight." She took me to a small room up one flight of stairs. "You can pick any bed you want. I think it is only you and one other man in here tonight. I have two men from Switzerland coming, too, but they will be in the other room. You look very tired. Are you okay?"

I laughed. "I am tired. I've been walking almost a month from Geneva. I think my body's had enough."

"You are going to Nice?"

"Yes."

"Don't worry," she said with a hand on my arm. "You will be swimming in the sea in less than a week."

Vincent and Bruno arrived half an hour later with Mary and her friends. A young couple who couldn't have been older than twenty arrived just before dinner. They were a few days into a cycling trip through France and Italy. They were camping mostly but had decided to splurge on a good meal and a bed tonight. The girl spoke perfect English—she'd learned from watching American TV. She found it impossible to believe that I had come all the way from America to hike through southeastern France. Had I been to Paris? Who comes to France and goes to Larche but not Paris? Don't you have mountains in America? Can't you hike in California? What does your family think? Are you happy to be almost finished? That last question caught me off guard. I hadn't considered that I was actually almost finished. Nice still felt impossibly far away. I told her I imagined I would be happy when I reached the sea but that I didn't know what I would do after. I didn't want to fly back home yet. And I had no idea what I would do for work. She thought the whole thing was hilarious.

"Do you like hiking?"

"Sometimes. I'm not very good at it though. As my friend Thomas can tell you."

Thomas told the story of my slip and fall to the table in French. He delivered it dramatically and the girl put her hand over her mouth. Vincent blew a long sigh of relief at the end and Bruno said that the same thing had happened to him a few years ago, and he had seriously hurt his knee.

"It's just bad luck," he said. "But don't push it."

21

Our group the next morning included Vincent, Bruno, Mary and her friends, Thomas, and myself. The ladies were in the lead, followed by the Swiss, then me, and Thomas at the rear. He sidled up to me after we'd been out for half an hour or so.

"*Ça va?*"

"*Ça va.*"

"Good."

"Do you know about the route today?" I asked.

"I never know."

"It's a lot of climbing."

"Every day is climbing."

"There are two cols."

"Two col, three col, four col. All the same."

"I wish I had your attitude. I can't stop studying the guide to see what's coming."

"I like surprises."

The path took its time moving out of Larche and into a long valley. We passed a sign marking the entrance to the Parc National du Mercantour that warned visitors against feeding the marmots by hand. As if on cue, scads of marmots materialized around us. They must have been waiting. It was like a marmot sanctuary (as if such a thing would ever be necessary, which it wouldn't, since marmots are to the Alps what squirrels are to my backyard, only more annoying because of their whistle). That's not to say I'm immune to their charms; I have dozens of pictures of marmots on my phone—marmots close up, marmots far away, marmots standing still, marmots running, marmots diving into burrows.

Half an hour into the park, one of the ladies stopped suddenly and pointed up to the hillside. Like children, we all stopped and looked to where she was pointing.

"Chamois," she whispered.

"Where?"

"I don't see it?"

"There. Up there!"

"By that tree?"

"I don't see anything."

"It's not a chamois. It's a bouquetin!"

"Point again."

"Are you sure?"

"I can't see anything. Only bushes."

"I see it! By the tree."

"No, it's not by the tree. It's lower."

"I don't see a tree. Where are you looking?"

"Get the binoculars."

"It's a bush."

"It is not a bush. Give me those binoculars."

"Never mind. It's a bush, not a bouquetin."

We took a break at Lac du Lauzanier after a couple of hours of difficult climbing. I was already tired, and nervous about a sharp new pain in my lower back that spiked up my spine with each swing of my right leg. The ladies showed no signs of slowing down. Vincent and Bruno had splintered off and started working their way around the lake and up the mountain. Thomas was stretched out on the grass with his shoes and socks off. He had an odd habit of taking his shoes and socks off no matter how short the rest was. Anxious, I told the group I was going up behind Vincent and Bruno and would see them at the top. I dug my headphones out of a forgotten pocket of my bag, cued up Miles Davis's *Kind of Blue* on my phone, and got back on the trail. Up to that point, I hadn't listened to any music while walking for fear of breaking some unwritten hiking rule and attracting dirty looks from other walkers, especially older ones. But now, for forty-five minutes I paid no attention to the path, the pain, or the mountains. I thought instead of the self-contained world inside the album, the way the harmonies stack on top of one another to create something from nothing, the fluidity of the players, the way the record takes its time. I thought of the old drummer back in New York, playing himself to death because it's what he does. I thought of the monks in the monastery; of my father in his car; of Bernard, and Monika, and Colin. I thought of the wide-open emptiness that waited for me at the end of this endless line through the mountains, and how curious it will be to have nowhere else to go.

I found the two Swiss asleep by another lake higher up. The path swung wide to the left and inched up a sheer wall of tiny slippery rocks. I sat down next to Vincent and got my guide out.

"Follow the path from a grassy slope onto boulder scree, which is easy if taken steadily, to reach an impressive rocky col." But what if it's not taken steadily? I thought. Also: "Note: Take care descending from the col as the limestone is badly fractured and blocks could fall." Then this: "The whole area is shaped by unstable geology, with crumbling . . ." I closed the book. The only not-terrible thing I read was that the col was the official border between the Alpes du Haute-Provence and the Alpes-Maritimes, the final department I would be passing through. There were no more mountains at the bottom of the Alpes-Martimes, only water.

Once everyone in our ragtag group had made it to the lake, we ate lunch and waited a few minutes for Thomas to take off his shoes and socks, rest a bit, and drink some water. The ladies told us they were going to sit by the lake for a while and urged us to go on. With Bruno in the lead, we took the col like astronauts in zero gravity. We moved slowly, the four of us, in lock-step and almost total silence. Even though the climb was steep and the sun directly over us, I didn't break a sweat. I heard my own breathing, my own heartbeat, the squeak of the straps on my bag, the crunching sound of feet on loose rocks in rhythm. Bruno whispered to himself, "*Belle ambiance.*" And Vincent said, "*Tranquille.*" We moved under a kind of spell. I don't know how long it took to climb to the col, probably no more than forty-five minutes, and the spell was broken by the loud cackle of a woman already at the top when we got there.

Vincent and Bruno found a point where the col hung over the descent and took turns craning their necks over it. I anxiously scanned for the path that led down, but couldn't find it, which meant either that there was no way off or that the path was hiding behind some rock, way too close to the edge of the col. I played it cool and agreed with everyone about how incredible the views were, saying things like, "*c'est bon*" and "*magnifique*," but I could barely stand to look.

Apparently, I really had developed a fear of heights after more than three weeks in the high mountains. And the stress of being that high was compounded when I reached back to scratch my shoulder and found the barbed end of a bee. I had never been stung before and it hurt like hell. Almost immediately, my finger started throbbing and I stared at it in disbelief. A bee sting? At nine thousand feet? Surely this was another sign. God, it hurt. All I could do was stare at my finger, which looked perfectly normal, and guess at the kind of bad luck it takes to get stung by a bee in such a place. There weren't even any flowers.

I expected the throbbing to die off after a few minutes, but it only got worse. I didn't mention the sting to the others. I just walked around like an idiot holding my own hand. With their fill of the view, Vincent, Bruno, and Thomas found the path (easily) and started down. As the slowest and most accident-prone, I went last. It was every bit as terrifying as I imagined it would be. The path was chopped into short, steep zigzags that threatened to send me falling clear down the mountain at every turn. I moved painfully, with my eyes on the ground and every muscle in my body tensed and ready for a spill. I shuffled down the mountain; it took forever. The guys were waiting for me at the end.

"*Ça va?*"

"*Ça va.*" I said. "*Je suis désolé. Lent.*"

"Slow is safe." Bruno said.

We cut across a meadow and crossed a dry riverbed. At an abandoned cabin just under the final col of the day, Vincent asked if I had a reservation in Bousieyas that night. I did not. My decision to take a chance on lodgings at every stop had become a bit of a joke by that point.

"Perhaps you should stay here then," he said. "There is some hay upstairs. For sleeping."

The gîte was full by the time we got there, but there was another just down the street. It was suggested I try that one. I walked down the road and asked if there was any room.

"We have only one guest tonight."

"That's crazy. The other gîte is full."

"Sometimes they are full and we are empty. Sometimes we are full and they are empty."

A few minutes later, I was marking up my notebook when I looked up and saw Thomas walking toward me with all his gear. It turned out he was the other guest that night. He'd nearly settled into the other place when they realized he had no reservation there and sent him here.

"The chef here is very good," he said.

"How do you know?"

"He works in a very good restaurant in the town." I didn't know which town he meant, but it didn't matter. Dinner that night was absurdly good—venison with mushrooms picked that day out of the woods, local cheeses, and some kind of homemade pie. We were joined at the last minute by a young couple from Brittany, Noah and Louise. On top of being handsome and athlete-fit, they were both doctors. They smiled at everything.

After dinner, Thomas and I hiked up a long set of stairs to the other gîte to say our farewells to Vincent and Bruno, who would be heading off in a different direction tomorrow toward Menton. Thomas briefly debated going with them. The route to Menton is supposed to be breathtaking and it goes through the Vallée des Merveilles. I couldn't follow the conversation, but in the end he decided to go on to Nice, which was one or two days closer. I suspect he was tired; we all were. And the final day is a magnet that, once you are close enough, draws you powerfully toward it. We drank to our success: for having made it all this way, for having walked through the rain, for being alive, for getting close to the end.

22

At a certain point, I must have stopped caring. I don't know when, exactly—maybe when I crossed into the Alpes-Maritimes —but all I could think about was the sea, the golden-brown vacationers on the beach, and how badly I wanted to be one of them. I lapsed into long daydreams of waking up in a hotel room under cool sheets, walking fifteen feet to the ocean, and not letting my feet touch the ground for days. I fantasized about moving as little as possible, about walking without the constant weight of my bag. I had gorgeous visions of my hiking shoes melting in a massive bonfire.

Which is perhaps why the final few days of my journey have blended into one long, monotonous slog through sun-dried grass, low hills, podunk hill towns, and blistering heat. I was over all of it and mindlessly, desperately winding down to the end.

Still, some moments shone brighter than others. From Bou-seiyas, Thomas and I hiked quietly up to a col, down into a valley, back up again to another col, and down into Saint-Etienne-de-Tinée, a mountain town with a population of close to two thousand people. Thomas had done the work of booking us at a gîte. We were the only guests that night. I told Thomas I needed to go into the city center and pick up a few supplies, mostly candy bars. I was eating my weight in chocolate since I figured I was burning thousands of calories just getting from one candy bar to the next.

The square was hemmed in by small shops, a church, a boulangerie, and the town hall. I picked up a pastry and sat down at a café for a coffee. I watched a swarm of birds—or bats—fly spirals around the church's bell tower. It was a holiday, but I couldn't figure out what was being celebrated. When the sun went down, a children's orchestra put on a performance. One of the pieces was especially beautiful, even in the small, nervous hands of children. Afterwards I went to look for the conductor to ask what it was, but he disappeared into the crowd before I could get to him. I can still hear fragments of the melody—pieces I'll hold onto for as a long as I can—and they bring me back immediately to that warm night with the bats (or birds) flying around and the smell of cigarette smoke and beer.

In the morning, Thomas pitched his plan. The walk from Saint-Etienne-de-Tinée to Auron, a ski center up in the mountains, was boring and mostly stuck to paved or dirt roads. We could save a couple of hours by taking a shuttle. From Auron, instead of going all the way to a refuge twenty miles away, we would split it into two short days. Afternoons had become dangerously hot, and according to the book, it was a nineteen-mile walk to the next refuge. It took very little convincing on Thomas's part. If he had suggested a shuttle to Nice, I probably would have agreed.

The van picked us up at around ten and dropped us in Auron twenty-five minutes later. Thomas wanted to find a swimming pool, and we agreed to meet in a couple hours to eat lunch in Auron. Since our stop was only two hours away, it all sounded great. I grabbed a seat under an umbrella at a café and said that I'd wait there but that he should take his time. I had plenty of reading to do. He came back half an hour later, having not found a single pool in the whole city.

"Let's get out of here," I said.

"To Roya?"

"Yes. It's hot."

"Very hot. We are near the sea."

"Not near enough."

We picked our way up a hill that had been dug out with mountain biking tracks. Bikers blasted down the mountain at what seemed to me very dangerous speeds and nearly knocked us down at least ten times. I couldn't think of a less glamorous way to die than by being hit by a cyclist after thirty days of walking through the Alps. Once, in Vietnam, I was hit by a motorcyclist when I was crossing the street. He knocked us both down and yelled at me for a full minute before he realized I wasn't under-standing a word he was saying (though it wasn't hard to guess), at which point he got back on his bike and drove off. When I told people the story, no one was impressed. Somehow *I* was the idiot for having gotten in the way.

We climbed to the col, took a few pictures of the view, and walked down to Roya, another hamlet that seemed too minute to actually exist. Outside the gîte, Thomas studied his maps while I read. We ate dinner that night with Noah and Louise under an unusually clear sky. Even in the south, the night sky was often cloudy, and in all the time I'd been walking I still hadn't seen the stars. When I mentioned this to Noah, he told me there would be a full moon that night, but it wouldn't be high enough to see until quite late. I was in the habit of collapsing into bed and falling asleep immediately after dinner to give my body as much time to rest as possible. At half past nine, I gave up waiting. The sky wasn't even dark.

I woke at four in the morning and climbed down from my top bunk to go to the bathroom. The door at the end of the hall had been left open, and the woods were lit up in a brilliant fluorescent white, as if our gîte were in the beam of a UFO. I walked down the hall to the door and paused for a moment before stepping through the threshold. Outside, the world was silver, drowned in moonlight. The sky was still cloudless, and the moon was so big and so bright I had to squint to look directly at it. It was light enough to walk in, I thought.

We woke early—a habit now. In my head is not a single memory of the walk that day, except for a moment on a high col. The lodgings at either end are clear as day, but what happened in between is almost completely blank. Not even the pictures look familiar. I have ways of piecing memories together, lining them up in the proper order and filling in the blanks, but nothing works for this day. I blame the blind spot on a kind of fatigue— from the walking itself, from the heat, from the monotony of the landscape (which probably wasn't monotonous at all, just overwhelming after thirty days). I know from the book what I was meant to have crossed: a bouldery streambed, grassy slopes, plenty of scree. The only thing I can picture is a marble stub of a memorial on a shoulder of Mont Mounier. The memorial was chipped and beaten. It had a date on it: January 14, 1936. The book notes that views of the sea are possible from that very point, but I don't think we saw the sea that day. The sky was too blue, or the sea too white, or my eyes too tired. If I had seen the sea, I would have remembered; it would have been the first time.

La stèle Valette was the last pass higher than eight thousand feet. Everything from there on would be considerably lower. The pictures I took of the descent look terrifying, the line of the path cutting across a near-vertical wall of tiny black stones. There is no grass, only a few sad clumps of brownish shrubs a little lower down. In one photo, Thomas is a hundred feet ahead on the trail. In front of him, the path extends in a perfect straight line until it simply disappears over the edge of a cliff. My heart beats a little faster just looking at it. Perhaps it's a good thing—a natural thing—that I don't really remember it.

The refuge, in the "hanging valley" of Longon, is part of a working farm with horses, cows, dogs, chickens, and donkeys. The beds were thin mattresses on the second level of a barn. I climbed a sketchy ladder to get up there and set my bag down. The mattresses barely fit under the slanted roof. Noah and Louise were there by the time Thomas and I arrived. Noah was napping outside with a grin on his face while Louise was soaking, wringing, and hanging their clothes. She had a smile on her face, too. Between the animals and the mountains and the smiling, it was very *Sound of Music*. They showed no signs of having walked as much as I did.

"Look," Noah said. "It's the German."

I looked past a handful of cows and saw a man approaching. He was wearing all black—black jeans, a black denim shirt, a black hat. The skin on his face was a ghostly white except for the patches of bright red.

"You made it," Noah said to the man, who was desperately pulling at his water.

"Yah. But I'm very tired. I must sit." He collapsed into a pile on the ground and dug around his bag for more water. He was in his fifties and had a soft, round face and short red hair. He stood up after a minute and apologized for being in such bad shape.

"It's very hot today. I'm not feeling well."

"Drink more water," Noah said.

"Yes. I need more water." He shuffled off to the fountain to refill his bottles.

"The German is in terrible shape," Noah said to me when he was out of earshot. "Every time I see him, he looks worse. But he won't give up. I think maybe he's walking from Germany."

It turned out he was not walking from Germany. He wasn't even German, but Belgian, and had been walking only for a week or so. But it didn't feel right, he said. He was struggling. Still, he said he would go to Nice, but it would be his last big walk.

We dined on veal, homemade cheese, pasta, and *socca* (a staple of Niçois cuisine and a welcome sign that we were close). I drank enough wine to make it difficult to climb the ladder to my bed and fell asleep immediately under a wooden support beam I banged my head on when I woke up the next morning.

The air was cool enough overnight to saturate everything outside, including my clothes, which I'd hung on a line to dry the night before. I put the wet clothes on and ate breakfast quickly with Thomas, Noah, and Louise. The book showed seventeen miles between Longon and the town of St. Dalmas. Noah and Louise pulled far enough ahead that we lost them entirely after only two hours. Thomas and I had used up every bit of conversation over the last few days, so we walked in near silence. By eleven the sun was so intense we had to take constant breaks to cool down, find shade, and drink water. Covering seventeen miles through the mountains in decent weather would be hard enough; in the coastal August heat, it was just stupid. We were losing altitude, too, which made the heat worse.

We passed through Roure, a small village of red-roofed houses clinging for dear life to the side of a hill. In Saint-Sauveur-sur-Tinée, which at five hundred meters was lower than I had been in many, many days, we stopped at a boulangerie to buy something to eat for lunch. While we were eating in the shade of a tree next to a fountain, the German stumbled up looking even worse than he had the day before. He drained and refilled his half-liter water bottle no less than five times in as many minutes.

"Are you okay?" I asked.

"Very hot. Very hot."

"It's a terrible day for walking."

"Very hot. Very hot."

"I will take the bus to St. Dalmas." Thomas said.

"Really?" I asked, genuinely surprised.

"Yes. It is a boring road from here. I am not interested."

But I didn't have the energy or the desire to argue with him. Any idiot could see it was a mistake to walk in this heat. But I only had a few days left, and taking a bus at this point would feel like cheating, not unlike taking the bus a month earlier from Thonon did.

"I'm going to walk," I said.

"Be careful."

"If you don't see me tonight, send someone to look." I was joking, but Thomas took me seriously.

"If you are tired, you can stop at Rimplas."

"See you tonight."

Nervously, I left Thomas and the German at the fountain, alone for the first time in days. The temperature was well over ninety and I had four hard hours of climbing ahead of me. I took a wrong turn out of the village and was good and lost within half an hour. I doubled back to find a route marker, but found none. Frustrated and weak from the heat, I sat for a long time under a tree and considered going back to the village to catch the bus. Another hour, I thought. Calm down, give it an hour. If I'm still hopelessly off-route, I'll turn back. Worst case scenario, I'll sleep in Saint-Sauveur-sur-Tinée. Or in my tent, which I still hadn't used. I followed a path up through the woods for forty-five min-utes before I saw a red-and-white flag painted on a rock. My clothes were soaked through with sweat, and I was running out of water. The path opened onto a road that had been cut out of a cliff. With no shade, the heat was punishing. I looked like one of those people who gets lost in the desert and wanders in circles with his clothes torn to rags and tied around his head. My steps were half steps and gained me only a few inches at a time.

I walked under the hard, drilling sun for over an hour. By the time I reached the gated hilltop town of Rimplas, I couldn't be totally sure it was real. I had the odd feeling of having wandered into a fairy tale. I passed a number of small chapels and asked an elderly man in a white suit where I might find water. There was a fountain next to the *mairie*, he said. The water there is very good. He asked if I was all right and walked with me to the fountain. I filled my one-and-a-half-liter bottle and drained the entire thing over my head. Then I refilled it and drank it down in greedy gulps. I refilled again and drank, slower this time, until I had put three liters of cold water into my body. A wasp hovered nearby, but even the insects had been made indolent by the heat. I sat next to the fountain for a long time before I tried to stand up. Once the water had revived me, I grabbed my pack, which felt like it was weighted with cinder blocks, and started down the mountain on a small dirt track. The trail dipped out of Rimplas before climbing for several hours through a series of uninteresting suburbs to St. Dalmas.

Noah's beaming grin was the first thing I saw when I found the gîte.

"You're alive."

"Barely," I said.

"We were wondering if we would see you again tonight. Thomas said you had a tent and you might camp in the woods or stay in Rimplas."

"I figured this would be our last night together, so I had to make it."

"Did you hear about the German?"

"Hear what?"

"He quit. He took the bus from Saint-Sauveur-sur-Tinée straight to Nice." He was practically laughing as he said this.

"Damn. He was so close. But he really did look terrible. Worse than me."

"Yes. I'm happy he quit and not you. The next days will be very hot, but once you are in Nice, you will forget everything."

Thomas joined us outside.

"*Ça va?*"

"*Ça va.*"

"The German. He quit."

"I heard. Big news on the trail."

"Too hot."

"It was very hot today. I must have drunk six or seven liters of water."

"It's probably not enough. Drink more tonight or you will be in pain tomorrow."

"I'm already in pain. I think my body is just done. My feet and legs hurt all the time now. And my lower back is starting to really worry me. My shoulders are sore pretty often, too."

"The pain is part of the adventure," Noah said. "Do you sail?"

"Like sail? On a boat?"

"Yes. Sail."

"No. I'm from Kansas."

"We took our daughter sailing around the world a few years ago. One year. Senegal, South America, the Caribbean. In storms, the ocean is very frightening. But it's important to have some adventure, I think."

"You crossed the ocean?"

"Twice."

"I don't think I could ever do that."

He brushed this off. "Anyone can. It's simply a matter of doing it."

St. Dalmas to Utelle. Utelle to Aspremont. Aspremont to Nice. Leaving St. Dalmas, I repeated these words in my head like a mantra, an incantation, something to meditate on, a groove to lock into. Three more days. Forty more miles. That's it. It had been a month since I left Geneva and the sea was finally close enough to feel, but still too far to actually see.

The primary hurdle of the day, other than the eighteen miles of walking, was the Brèche du Brec, a rocky col, which, from the description in the book, sounded like the place where I was sure to finally slip and fall to my death. It came later in the day, after six and a half hours of walking. We were blessed with good, cloudy weather that kept the temperature down, but we were both tired. We kept our eyes on a storm that was gathering strength to the west. Storms in this area, where the warm air off the sea meets the mountains, are frequent and can be violent. Around eleven, high up in the woods, we were swallowed by clouds so thick I couldn't see Thomas, who was only a few feet ahead of me. For thirty minutes we were pummeled by rain, thunder, and lightning. We kept on, like sad soldiers no longer interested in the whims of the weather. Then, as suddenly as the storm had appeared, it was gone.

We passed a group of women saddled with baskets. They were out picking berries. And later, a road crew that was paving a backcountry route and some men huddled around a truck engaged in what looked to be a vaguely illicit deal for mushrooms. We ate lunch on tree stumps surrounded by horses.

When we reached the Brèche du Brec, the trail worked steeply up around a crumbling rocky pyramid that was exposed on all sides. From every turn, the path looked like it simply dropped off the mountain after ten feet. The climbing went on forever. At the top, a ramp led up to a cliff face where I had to cling around a corner and drag myself to some more crumbling steps that led down off the mountain. Thomas was remarkably unbothered by how precarious our situation was. Or he was too tired to care. We made it up and over without incident, but I was checked out. I swore I'd never put myself through it again. It was exhausting feeling so tightly wound and so worn out at the same time, like being pulled apart at the seams.

The only available beds in the hilltop town of Utelle were on the second floor of a small apartment attached to the church. The church itself was old, hundreds of years old, but the apartment was clean and empty. I slept on the upper bunk with my head a foot from a creaky window that looked out over the hills. The cool air blew in like a soft breath from the sea, salty and clean. Two days, I thought. Only two more days. Utelle to Aspremont, Aspremont to Nice. Utelle to Aspremont, Aspremont to Nice. I mouthed the names to myself in bed. Utelle. Aspremont. Nice.

Thomas and I left early the next morning, both of us complaining to each other about various aches and pains. Thomas's knees were killing him, he said.

"Mine too," I said. "It was the descent yesterday. Too hard."

"Perhaps, I will not walk all the way."

"What do you mean? I can't carry you."

"I may go only to Aspremont. I think from Aspremont, the walk is not so interesting. So if there is a bus, I may take the bus."

I didn't think he was serious. From Aspremont, it was only three or four hours to Nice. Why would anyone quit when they've made it so far?

"I would love a bus," I said. "But I have to walk."

"Yes. I understand. But be careful. I think you are tired."

"You have no idea."

We passed a small chapel. A sign inside dated it to 1686, but Thomas said it was probably older. It was the size of a small closet and bursting with the collected offerings of thousands of pilgrims—flowers, candles, statuettes, newspaper clippings. I wanted to leave something, to offer a piece of myself to the mountains, but I had nothing to give.

In Levens, halfway to Aspremont, we ate lunch and Thomas called ahead to reserve beds. I tried to follow the phone conversation, but none of the French words were finding their English counterparts inside my dulled brain. After he hung up, Thomas explained that Aspremont was full and that we would have to find another option. We could stay here, in Levens, he said, but it would be a longer walk the next day.

"What are our other choices?"

"We have none."

"So we'll have a short day today, and a long day tomorrow."

"Yes. But I will take the bus tomorrow."

"From here?"

"I am finished," he said.

"Really? Are you sure? It's only one more day."

"You should finish alone. It's better."

"I don't mind the company."

"I am tired. My legs are in pain. We are mostly out of the mountains, and I am not interested in walking through the city."

I considered trying to convince him, but what was the point? He'd gotten his fill. He was done. I was done, too. The only difference was that I still had many hours of walking ahead of me. I am trying to remember, now, if I thought about taking the bus, too. I'm sure I did, but I can't recall. Or maybe I didn't. Maybe I was so committed by then that it truly didn't occur to me. I like to think that's the case. But I'm not sure. I am a quitter by nature. I always find the easy way out, even if it's extra work. I avoid challenges. I have no real interest in "pushing myself," in "broadening my horizons." I am not a hard worker like my father, or my mother, or my brother, or my sister, or my grandfather. The path of least resistance has always been my favorite path.

So, again, I had to wonder: what was I doing here? And if, after all these miles, I'm still asking myself the question, does the answer even matter?

23

I like to think that I've always loved walking, but it wasn't until I left home that I actually discovered it. The thing is, no one walks in Kansas City; it simply doesn't register as an option for getting from one place to another. The school I went to for my entire childhood, for example, was less than a mile from my house. We lived on top of a hill and I could see the building from my window. Still, I never walked. No one did. Not there and not back. For thirteen years, we drove the five minutes down and the five minutes up every day. I reckon my city, and to an even greater extent my suburb, was never built for walking. It was built for driving and for parking. Perhaps it's the exaggerated distances that separate everything that make moving on foot so unappealing, the way a mile feels like ten because there is nothing to look at. There is so much space in my part of the country that it feels like a waste not to use it.

But I also like to think walking is in my blood. We are rootless wanderers by nature, my family, having been expelled from many places many times over the years. If you ask anyone older than I where we came from, the answer will either be Russia or Romania. Together, Russia and Romania make up over an eighth of all the land on the planet, which makes the answers both a safe bet and completely meaningless. We are untraceable, really. There are no records of our family in any city outside of the United States, yet we've only been here for two or three generations. Our surname only goes back one generation. My father's father grew up with a different last name, but no one is sure anymore exactly what it was. We are not, historically speaking, bound to any single place on Earth.

And then there is my great-uncle, an eccentric pizza-chef-turned diet-guru, who was, for the second half of his life, a world-class walker. In New York, where he lived for many years, you could spot him on one of his strolls cruising up and down Fifth Avenue in a patchy Madras sport coat, white 501s, and rainbow-laced Nikes. He was famous for, among other things, being fat, or rather having once been fat, and for the staggering amount of food he could still eat when he was no longer fat. In his twenties, he'd lost half his body weight through a combination of extreme dieting and obsessive walking. People still called him Fats, a nickname he had his whole life even when he was as thin as a twig. When he left New York and moved back to Kansas City in his late fifties, he took to walking laps around the inside of a dying shopping mall. He became a kind of de facto leader of a gang of nylon besuited senior citizens who had to practice their ambulations in semisecret. Toward the end of his life, when dementia had disconnected him from the rest of the world and rendered him speechless, he could still walk—so deep is the instinct.

In New Orleans, where I attended college, one of my favorite things to do was start walking back uptown from the French Quarter on the streetcar line. This was in the months right after the hurricane, when the city was staggering to stand itself up and nothing worked right. I would take off and see how long it took for the streetcar to catch up. If it came early, I'd hop on and ride home, but if I made it far enough, say past Napoleon, I'd walk the whole way and get back to my house at the river bend sheathed in a film of sweat, exhausted but happy. New Orleans is a great city for walking because none of the streets run in a straight line. The city is dictated by the Mississippi River, and the river couldn't care less about grid systems, traffic, or efficiency. Even the relatively straight blocks of the French Quarter feel topsy-turvy, as if bent by the river's gravity. It's easy to get lost there, to explore.

When I think about it, all the cities I've loved share this wonderland walking quality: Cairo, where it can take hours to move five hundred feet; Osaka, with its hidden underground worlds and endless shopping arcades; even New York, where walking is perhaps the only activity that doesn't cost any money. And Belgrade—where I live for the time being—particularly the old Jewish Quarter, which is small but feels large because it is old and soaked in history.

I like to think, too, that walking in the mountains was a natural step, so to speak, for me—a necessary one, as if I'd wandered out of a city, out of my life, and I was crossing the Alps to get back.

The explorer Robert Falcon Scott, frozen, frostbitten, exhausted beyond imagination, starving, and with the full knowledge that he had no hope for survival, found the strength to write in his diary on perhaps the last day of his life. Having been beaten to the South Pole by Amundsen's team, he was within eleven miles of the next depot on the return journey when he and his team were pinned down for days by blizzards. Only in the final few lines of his diary does Scott admit that he can't record anymore: "We shall stick it out to the end, but we are getting weaker, of course, and the end cannot be far. It seems a pity, but I do not think I can write more." There may not be a more heartbreaking line in the history of exploration. By contrast, here is the final line of my diary: "A day from Nice. Feet still hurt. Legs hurt, especially knees. Had dinner (pizza, gross) with Thomas, who is." Who is . . . what? I don't know. I stopped writing there, midsentence. That's it, the very last words in my notebook.

I have no notes or photos from Levens to Nice, either, only organic memories. It may have been a conscious decision to not put the day in a box. To allow, instead, my mind to hold on to what it would and let go of the rest. It could also have been laziness. I don't remember. In any case, I've etched a version of it onto my brain in the months since—and for better or worse, it's all I have.

I leave Levens early, as soon as I wake up. Thomas is asleep, so I tiptoe out of our hotel room and pack my bag outside. Breakfast doesn't start for another hour, but a woman working in the kitchen sees me and brings a cup of a coffee and a croissant. When I offer to pay, she waves my money away. It's an auspicious start to a monumental day. But I try not to think of that. I remind myself to take it slow, to not rush, to absorb everything I can, to make it count. It's not a race; it never was.

I take my dish back into the kitchen and thank the woman again. I tell her, because I have to tell someone, that it's my last day, that I've been walking for over a month, and that *today is the last day*. She asks how I feel, and I say I have no idea, weird. She asks if I walked alone. Yes and no, I say. She asks if I have food for the day, and even when I say yes, she packs me a small lunch of breakfast pastries and slices of meat. I feel like I'm going to burst with gratitude.

I pick up the path outside the city center, but it doesn't really leave the city. Maybe this is what Thomas meant by boring. I stay on roads and pass a large field where a few people are walking their dogs. Finally, after an hour or so, I see a sign that pushes that path into some trees. There are dozens of paths and they crisscross. I assume they all lead to the same place, but I'm careful with the markings, too careful maybe because I'm only looking at the ground. The climb is gentle, but I feel it in my calves, which pisses me off. When I arrive at a clearing where the land feels like it's leveling out, I look up and see the sea. The Mediterranean. There it is, like it's nothing. The sea, I think. But it's hard to process. It has been so abstract until now that I'm not prepared for it. Just the day before, Thomas asked me if I could hear the seagulls. I couldn't hear anything then except the woods. And now I'm looking at the sea, and I could cry, the way you cry when you don't know what else to do.

In Aspremont, where I was supposed to sleep the night before, I buy a banana and sit for a few minutes on a bench. It's hot, but the heat doesn't bother me. I can't get the image of the water out of my head. It seems impossible and cruel that I still have several hours of walking left before I reach it. But the book doesn't lie, and even though I feel close enough to literally taste it, I don't get my hopes up. I still have one final climb, a short one, before the path plummets over two thousand feet down into Nice.

On maps, the Alps look a little like a talon scraping east across five countries. They swoop down out of Austria, through Switzerland where they skirt Lake Geneva, and on into France, where the claw curls back into Italy just east of Monaco. In Aspremont, I am just south of the curl, which is to say I am essentially out of the mountains. It feels like it and it doesn't. The shift was slow enough that I hardly noticed it. The terrain is rugged, rocky, and covered in thatchy trees and shrubs that scratch my legs sometimes when I'm not paying attention. But the peaks, when I look back at them, are far away and impossibly high. I am in a middle ground, a no-man's-land that is neither mountain nor sea nor city, and even though I am walking out of them, the Alps are terrifying to look back at. It reminds me of something I read about people blindfolding themselves when they passed through the high peaks. The mountains were so horrifying that no one would cross them with their eyes open.

I climb Mont Chauve, which is harder than I want it to be, but as soon as it's over, I miss it. I follow the trail onto the western flank of the hill and the city of Nice explodes in Mediterranean whites and golds and reds below me. It extends far into the valley toward me, growing browner as it does. It's my first time seeing the city but I'm too anxious to stop and look at it. In a few minutes, it doesn't matter because I'm in it. I'm passing a school on a sidewalk. I'm crossing a highway on an overpass. I'm winding through small neighborhood streets lined with garish houses and expensive cars. I lose track of the markers, which apparently lead to a small park in the center of the city. But I'm not interested in a park. I want the sea. So I set a southern course and stick to it. My feet are killing me, I realize, because I've barely taken a break those few minutes in Aspremont. I've been walking for hours, and I can't bring myself to stop. I'm moving fast, too, despite the pain and the weight on my back and the sun.

I drop out of the hilly neighborhoods north of the city onto a main street, and for the first time in weeks the ground is truly flat. There are people everywhere. I can't imagine how ridiculous I look in my mountain clothes. It's almost embarrassing to be out here, strolling down the avenue after a month in the mountains. I can't shake the feeling that everyone is staring at me, which only makes me move faster.

North of the train station, I pick up Avenue Jean Médicin, which I know from having studied a map of Nice leads directly to the water. It's the final stretch of the final stretch, and none of it feels real. Not the city, not the people, not the cafés or the shops or the statues or the tram. The buildings are all candy-colored in the afternoon sun and suddenly the pavement is a dizzying mosaic of black-and-white tile, like a giant chessboard. I cross the Place Masséna and the road dead-ends at a fountain, beyond which there are several small streets branching out, like doors number one, two, and three in a game show I don't want to be on. I don't even stop moving. I take the street that's closest, Rue de l'Opéra. I know I'm near because I can actually hear the sound of the sea, the unmistakable pink noise of the sea washing up against Europe.

The street is only a block long, but because of the angle, my view is blocked. The first thing I notice when I get to the end of it is the Neuf Lignes Obliques, a monument a hundred feet high, made of nine steel beams leaning against one another. It looks like a mountain made of metal and it's impossible to process. The second thing I notice is that behind the monument, there's no city, no buildings—there's nothing. I cross the promenade quickly with my stomach in my throat. The sea is

no more than a hundred feet away. I take a flight of stairs down
to the sand, which isn't sand really, but small rocks. I make
myself stop for a moment, force myself to slow down. I drop
my pack and take off my shoes and socks. I inhale a deep breath
and make myself think all the way back to the first step I took
that morning in La Chapelle D'Abondance. I take a single step
and close the gap between myself and the water by two feet. I
take another. And another. And a dozen more. But the closer I
get to the water, the more impossible it seems that I'll ever be
able to touch it.

I am a walking illustration of one of Zeno's paradoxes, the
one that says I can never get to the end of the path because there
are an infinite number of half-distances, and quarter-distances,
and eighth-distances, and so on that I would have to cover first.
So I stop inches short of the water and see if, maybe, it will come
to me. I came all this way, I think. It's the least you can do. And
the water does come close, but then it recedes, almost timidly. I
don't move. I wait. It gets closer every time, millimeters closer,
but it doesn't touch. There is a ship on the horizon, just sitting
there on the hard line where the water meets the sky. At first it
looks like it isn't moving but it is, barely, like the hour hand of a
clock or clouds on a windless day.

I stand there for ages, squinting out to sea until I can no longer tell where it ends and the sky begins. Everything in my field
of vision is an expanding blur of whitish-blue blinding me from
the center outward. So it comes as something of a shock when I
look down and find myself ankle-deep in the Mediterranean. I
reel, like a boxer falling toward the floor before he even knows he's
been hit. The rush of the water throws me off for a minute, and I
have to catch myself or I'll topple. I walk out farther to try to find
some balance. I'm knee-deep, then waist-deep, then neck-deep in

thick, warm blue water. I take one last breath before I'm released, and I let go of the land with my feet, let go of the mountains, of the path, of everything I've carried with me. It's the last second, and I realize, too late, all the things I meant to do—the peaks I meant to notice, the lakes I meant to swim in, the skies I wanted to sleep under, the stars I meant to gaze at, the people I'd hoped to meet, the questions I wanted to ask. I remember the promise I made to myself—to go back and walk those first two days I had skipped when I took the bus to La Chapelle-d'Abondance instead—and I know not only that it won't ever happen, but also how absurd it was to think it might. I wonder if anything has changed since I left Geneva, if I'm any different than I was five hundred miles ago—but the thought is cut short by the sheer, muscular force of the water, and I let it absorb me, pull me down, away from everything, out into the Bay of Angels, until I'm suspended several feet above the ocean floor and only a few inches below sky. After a month of measuring my distance from the top of the sea, I am finally below it. I try to hold myself perfectly still, to not move a muscle. I drift underwater like that for as long as my lungs allow, feeling entirely weightless, held together not by any internal architecture but by the sea itself—gone, for the moment at least, from the surface of the earth.

Acknowledgments

Thanks to:

All of my walking companions, but especially Colin, with whom I would gladly walk another five hundred miles (but hopefully not in the rain).

The book—*The GR5 Trail* by Paddy Dillon (Cicerone), a staggeringly practical resource for walking the route I walked. To anyone even considering the trek, I highly recommend buying a copy. It's small, weather-resistant, and bursting with information. It is every bit the guide that my book fails miserably to be.

Cory, Kristin, Sara, Jason, and Herman for knowing full well what I was getting myself into and still supporting this project from the start. Your encouragement and feedback were invaluable.

Clarie and Jeff, for graciously putting me up in their home in the hills above Monaco and turning an already fairy-tale year into the stuff of legends. For a month, I was lucky enough to live under the Trophée des Alpes and pretend the victory was mine.

Saša, who found me wandering the streets of Belgrade and, for reasons I still don't fully understand, gave me not only a place to live, but encouragement, two dogs, family, food, coffee, and, above all, friendship.

Andrew, Ragnar, Lane—old friends, creative partners, personal heroes.

The entire Skyhorse team—the hardest working group of people in publishing—and my editor, Kim Lim, in particular, for her patience, close reading, and guidance.

The wonderful staff and unrivaled coffee at The Roasterie Café in Leawood, Kansas, where the vast majority of this book was written.

And, finally, my family—Mom, Pop, Zachary, Sara, Seymour, Marsha, Sharon, and Joel—eight of the most incredible, funny, creative, independent, hardworking, generous people I have ever met. Simply put, none of this, nor anything else I've ever accomplished in my life, would have been possible without you, and I'm forever grateful for your support, encouragement, and love.

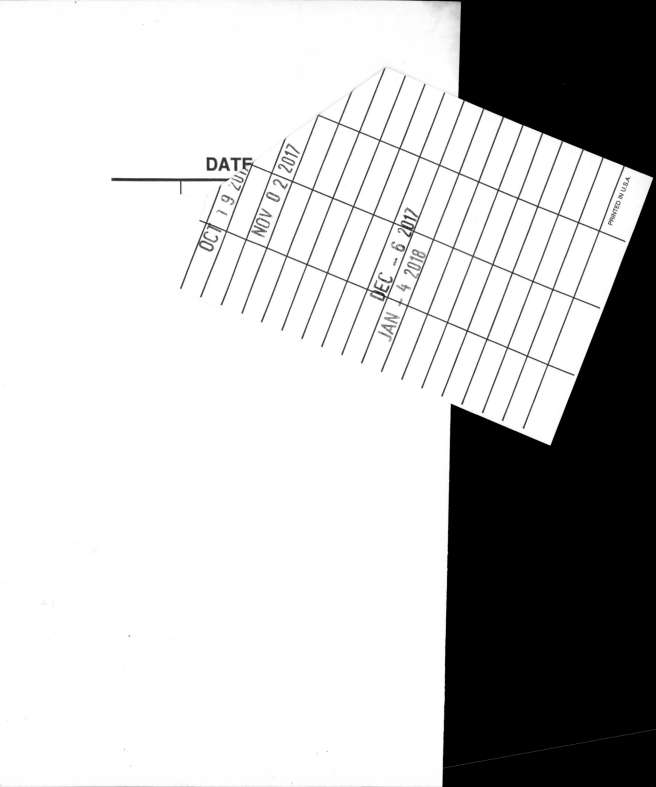

DATE

OCT 19 2017

NOV 0 2 2017

DEC - 6 2017

JAN - 4 2018

PRINTED IN U.S.A.